Walking
on
Forbidden
Waters

Walking
on
Forbidden
Waters

Sir Alexender Lorenzo

WALKING ON FORBIDDEN WATERS

First Edition, Second Impression 2018
978-1-928325-57-4

Contact Information:
ALEXANDER LORENZO
Cell: 063 362 3443
Whatsapp: 063 422 7746
Email: siralexlorez@gmail.com
Facebook: http://www.facebook.com/www.walkingonforbiddenwaters.co.za
Instagram: https://www.instagram.com/walking_on_forbidden_waters

Layout Design and Typesetting by Zion Publications
Published by Zion Publications

Contact Information:
Email: info@zionintl.com
Website: www.zionintl.com

CONTENTS

FOREWORD

No one can deny the fact that there are so many books published by different publishing houses, written in different perspectives. An amazingly large number of authors are concentrating basically on writing books about the world and its relationship to mankind, books on finances, world wars, health and some, encompass on religion. This book however concentrates on each and every individual, and their relationship to the outside world. The following could be considered to be a true story, as the pages within will be a combination of my personal life experiences and events. This book could serve as a teaching manual, teaching *God's* Children endurance and perseverance in any predicament, hardship, austere situation and whatever else, that may stand between them reaching success. The Christian world must be made aware that being Children of *God*, does not necessarily mean their lives will always be filled with joyful atmospheres, that they will always have plenty, and everything go according to their specifics. But rather be aware, that times of trouble will come, even the Bible warns us about this.

There is going to be times, whereby you are going to face tribulations, pain and sufferings, but even through this, you must endure and persist up to the end. For it is written: *"Weeping may endure for a night, but joy cometh in the morning."(Psalm 30:5)*

This book is going to prophesy to you, reveal the secrets of *God* the *Father* unto you. It is filled with astounding mysteries about the Word of *God*. As a result of trials and tribulations, most Christians have ceased to believe in *God*, actually their faith has run dry, but this book is going to rekindle the faith you had, before trouble crossed your path. Many people today are sinking into the thralldom of poverty, because they allowed the socio-economic upheavals in today's world, to determine their state of mind as well as their lifestyle. This book could enable you to turn adversities into advantages, when faced with sombre times. It could help Christians remain prisoners of hope, unleashing courage and perseverance to *God's* Children. It's not just another book. It's filled with astounding gold nuggets, assisting one in how to live a satisfied life. It describes the temporary and permanent perspectives, for each and every time you have to make a decision in life, based on either of the two!!

MY LIFE STORY

ALEXANDER LORENZO ZEPHANIAH

I am a young man who was born, deep down the southern region of Africa, in motherland Zimbabwe. Abandoned by my mother at birth, I was raised by adoptive parents who were Rastafarians. Dedicated to Rastafarianism at age 3, I never had even the slightest opportunity to attend school. I came from a very rough background. I hated life the very day I came out of my mother's womb, up until the time I got born again. My stepmother always tried to kill me, since the day I started writing. I was five at the time. I wrote down in poetic form and short stories, all the things troubling me. I sensed writing was the deposit *God* placed inside me. At age 14, my stepmum attacked me with an axe. I was comatose for 7 months. A head procedure was performed, thereafter l suffered memory loss. When l was discharged from hospital, I didn't know who I was or what happened to me. I actually started off afresh, learning my name and to speak properly, similarly to the way a baby develops.

A year after my recovery, I was hit by a big haulage truck. I broke my left hand and right leg, but still I didn't die! The woman tried everything in her power to take my life. She didn't understand that it is only the One who gives life that has power to take it back, and it's none other than *God Almighty*. Never the less she didn't stop there, early 2005 she cooked me a very delicious meal, something she had never done before. *God* works in ways invisible to the naked eye. I didn't eat that meal, not due to a lack of appetite. My beloved younger sister was also hungry, so I offered her my meal. I watched as my own blood sister died in my place, she passed away in my arms. I cried bitterly for as bound by the power of blood, as we naturally were, all else brought us closer, even making us one. She was not only my sister, but I took her to be a mother, friend, and colleague, but above all she was my inspiration.

I blamed myself for her death even today I still believe that I killed my own sister. But, I accept *God* allowed her to die in my place, for a specific reason. I might not have understood it then, but deep down inside me I sensed it was *God's* will. I had no reason to stay on in that place. I couldn't bare the agony, pain, stress and the despair I was enduring. My stepparents always asked me to leave, and after my sister's burial, I decided it was time for me to go, but where would I go?

I became a street urchin, ending up getting involved in crime and drug abuse. I did so many things, if I am to share all the details, not a single person may believe it. I did the cruelest things one could imagine, broke so many hearts, while trying to drown my own sorrows. I was locked up in prison several times, until *God* caused me to be cast down, only then I sought His face. I got born-again in September 2008, at the Waters of Life Ministries. Since that day I persisted in prayer and fasting, and *God* performed many miracles in my life.

God gave me the privilege to attend school. One of the greatest miracles is that I managed to understand and pass Grade 12, without passing any other grades. I want to thank *Pastor Innocent Sibanda* who adopted me as his son, for everything he has done for me. I know it was divine appointment orchestrated by *God*; that I was going to call him Dad, and for that I am filled with an attitude of gratitude. I am a very difficult guy to understand. I may look 'simple,' but I am extremely hard to 'get.' It is not because I am smart or intelligent, but because I am called and anointed by *God* to do what I do.

My deepest fear is not that I am insecure or inadequate. My deepest fear is that I am powerful beyond measure. I ask myself who am I to be talented, intelligent and brilliant? Actually, who am I not to be? I am a Child of *God*. Playing small can never save the world. There is nothing enlightening about shrinking for the sake of others. I am not to blame if other people feel insecure around me. I am meant to shine! I was born to make manifest the glory of *God* within me. It's not only inside me, but inside everyone. As I make my own light shine, I subconsciously give others permission to do the same. I am liberated from my own fears, my presence automatically liberates others. I thank *God* because He didn't create in me '*a Spirit of fear but of boldness and a sound mind.*' *(2 Timothy1:7)* My life and future are secure in *God's* hands.

TO GOD BE ALL THE GLORY!

DEDICATION

To my beloved sister, *Lorraine:*
Blood is thicker than water. You are the greatest force behind
this book. Death came between you and I, but never has it
really managed to separate us. In all walks of life, through thick
and thin, I will always hold onto the memory of you in my
heart. You were a sister, mother and friend to me. You are the
motivation behind the writing of this book. Thank you so much,
my beloved sister. May your soul rest in eternal peace, until we
meet again in the afterlife!

ACKNOWLEDGEMENTS

To my father, *Apostle Innocent Sibanda*:
You are the greatest man alive, the wisest ever known, a rightful king to me, who should sit upon a throne. For when I was in darkness, you have been my guiding light. When all things went wrong, you put my world right, when I lacked knowledge, you continued to impart knowledge upon my life. I would not have written this book without your inspiration. Thank you so much Apostle. I wena *kaPasila, Dawuduna, Phothophotho, uMhlathi ongahlulwathambo, iSibindi esehlulamadoda esihanqile.* You are a true servant of God, I salute you!

To my mother, *Pastor Litracy Sibanda:*
You are a woman who always holds her head high. You possess stamina, beauty and courage, that all would admire. Even your love and happiness inspires one. Your beauty shines from inside out; it flows like a journey on a long route. You are the first woman who has shown me motherly love. This book would be

WALKING ON FORBIDDEN WATERS

incomplete if your name is not mentioned. Thank you so much my angel mother, all that I am, or wish to be, I owe to you, *Ndlovukazi!*

To The Woman I thought *God* Had Given Me, *Nicoletta Mayila!* I made you a priority in my life when I was just an option in yours but I thank you for betraying me, it was painful but worth it.

I thank you my little prince *Preshen:* Although you used to cry through the night, that did not stop me from writing this book, instead it gave me a reason to stay awake, and I could keep on writing, until the very last page!

I would have not done justice, if I neglect to thank *Pastor Thabang Mogano*, my brother in Christ, and his beautiful wife. They played a major role towards the publishing of this book. Not forgetting *Prophet Musa. K Zondo* and his wife, Nhlanhla Skhosana,

Pastor Byron Mhaka, Wilfred Khumalo, Nash Dube and many other wonderful men and women of the Well of Life Ministries, who contributed towards the success of this book. I cannot mention all of you by name, even so my prayer is that *God* may always remember you, because of your love towards me, and may He reward you greatly!

INTRODUCTION

Everything that happens or conspires comes into being due to a specific reason. I am writing this book, because of a net force driving me to this extent. I faced austere times, predicaments and also passed through the bondage of poverty, as well as being at the verge of giving up.

God challenged me to rise back to my feet again. A wise man is one who falls down seven times, but still rises to face the enemy once more. God said that I cannot function at His junction, if I allow socio-economic upheavals to control my life, as well as my state of mind. I learnt that the 'greatest' miracle of all things is prayer. I had only to turn mentally to God, and at once felt a force that poured into me from somewhere, into my soul, my whole being. What was it? Where from would I, an insignificant young man, tired of life, receive this strength that renewed and saved me, elevating me above all earth? It came from outside me, and there exist no worldly force which could resist it.

In this book I will lay it plain how prayer helps us build a stronger relationship with God, and a robust Christian life. I will also aim to teach you how to change your problems into projects, by implementing and following the principles found in the Word of God!

CHAPTER 1

TURNING PROBLEMS INTO PROJECTS!

It is really true that life will never be fair, unless someone else is fair to it first. I was in a predicament that caused me to go into paranoia. I couldn't distinguish between fact and truth, and no one could convince me to let go of the pain I was experiencing. I was in deep agony, too much to bear. I morbidly thought God had forsaken me. Most humanitarian careers lead the soul to a sense of *God.* Being loved, being a parent, taking on heavy responsibility, encountering death, even succeeding in life. Such events shake us out of our superficiality, triviality as we are brought face to face with reality, discovering the divine element of life. What more could be said about pain, poverty, suffering, trials and tribulations?

It will be true for many people that they need to be broken before they meet *God.* They will be subjected to long periods of suffering, agony and pain. It may be physical pain, loneliness, a wounded heart, the loss of dear ones, or cramped circumstances.

It may come through failure or through the fact that the thing we hold dear is frigidly refused us. I experienced pain, agony, suffering and rejection that confused me, and led me to backslide. I developed a sense of instability, because I thought *God* was no more controlling my life. If He was, then why was He allowing me to go through such a rough period of time, where no one was siding with me? I couldn't help, but shed tears day and night, for I had been refused somebody who was so dear to me. I was so tormented. My love was spurned; even my friends failed and deserted me. I clearly understood one thing: I was entering and learning a new phase of communion with God.

I believe I have an almost unanimous verdict from the people who are standing behind me. Literally, the only proof that anyone is in divine communion, is his love for other people. I magnified my pain, attempting to emphasise my own importance as a person, upon whom something unheard of descended. It seemed some spirit subtly suggested to me: *"The one really interesting thing about you is the magnitude of your agony."* Yet it remained real agony none the less, and life for me became a pale, narrow, sombre thing. But, I knew if I could manage to look beyond my pain, *God* was waiting for me. He waited not to remove the pain, but to share and sweeten it, till it changes its character.

I would have a drink with Him of that chalice, with Him who bears the full burden of the world's agony. Those who thus drink with God, pass into God's world; "a large and lovely world." But, I had little faith, even though I knew the Scriptures; I continued living in despair and sorrow. I spent sleepless nights plagued by morbid nightmares. This became part of my daily routine. I couldn't prevent myself falling asleep, but I wished that I could never sleep again for as long as I live! If only *God* had taken my life and spared my sister, I maybe wouldn't have suffered depression and stress. I began questioning God, why He allowed such despair and agony into my life.

I was totally convinced He had a good, vital reason for everything taking place in my life. God wouldn't allow such a great deal of pain to afflict me for no reason. I cried dry tears in my heart, carried a heavy load, and travelled on a lonely road. It's like I ceased to exist. It's going to sound a bit hysterical, if I use the phrase 'extinct' Why was I supposed to lead this kind of life? I loved but was not loved in return. I gave but did not receive in return, planted but reaped nothing. Worst of all, I prayed but none of my prayers were answered.

My life was like a paradox, for what I wanted I did not get, what I got I did not enjoy, and what I enjoyed was not permanent. Love is a mystery, for it takes two to tango. But, the truth is, love is a divine and pure gift from God, why then does it apply only to a chosen few? I longed to be loved, yet it was unreciprocated. I longed for someone to make me believe that love really exists, and would put back a smile on my face again. If only love had sight, then it wouldn't hurt, but the fact that it's blind, is the reason why the world is filled with such cruelty and heartlessness.

I didn't understand why the world turned so heartless, filled with apartheid, terrorism, confusion, crying and the gnashing of teeth. I started referring to the world as the new 'Sodom and Gomorrah,' for it was fast deteorating from Christianity to Atheism. I wished and hoped that *God* would come down Himself and bring the whole world to salvation and justice. If the world wasn't fighting for peace, but rather equal rights and justice, it would rotate around an atmosphere saturated with pure love and humanity. But, the more victimisation is upon it, the more foolish it becomes. People assume they are justified by their emotions, not realising that they are missing the whole point of being alive. Instead, they are condemned by their own decisive lusts and desires.

For me to change my problems into projects, I had to take a leap of faith – that 'crazy' type of faith. I started believing that nothing is impossible with *God.*

'God resists the proud, but gives grace to the humble.' (James 4:6)

When you build your faith strong in God's Word, you will neither cry nor be cast down in austere times. The Bible states that as long as we are in this world trouble is coming our way. No one is exempted from this Scripture, whether Christian or Atheist, one way or the other you're going to be faced with trouble. The question is: "How are you going to trouble those troubles?" We walk in a world that is strange and unknown, and in the midst of a crowd we could still feel lonely. We aren't alone; it's only that our sight is darkened by pain and despair.

Many times people fail in life, not because they plan to, but due to the prevailing economic problems experienced in their irrespective countries. We are living in the last days where all hell has broken loose. There is too much war, famine, sickness, suffering, torment, crying and radically increasing crime and corruption. You blame yourself, because you think all these predicaments, trails, tribulations, problems and austere times are a result of your personal wrong doings. You assume that you are suffering now because of your sins, but what does the Bible teach?

In *John 9:1-3* the disciples asked *Jesus* whether it was the blind man who sinned or his parents, for him to be blind. But *Jesus* proved them wrong and told them that it was neither the man nor his parents that sinned, but that happened so that the glory of *God* could be manifested through the man's blindness. Thus, not all suffering, pain and despair you're enduring is an outcome of your sins, however, all those things are coming to pass, that the glory of *God* could be manifested in your life.

You're hungry now, there is no food on your table and you don't have money, you don't even know what to do, but *God* wants you to know, for Him to be called *'Jehovah Jareh,'* one has to first experience lack. He cannot be called *'Rapha'*- the Healer when one is not sick, cannot be called your *Father* when you have never accepted Him as one. In times of trouble, as a Child of *God*, the spirit of discernment is vital, the ability to discern between the restraints, every time. Don't allow yourself to be cast down. A present day problem is that Christians place too much faith into material things; therefore they lack faith where it comes to the things of *God*. It is so sad when you find Christians, who believe *God* to be a type of genie you rub, and miracles begin to manifest.

No one ever wakes up early in the morning, and pray in tongues before opening their taps. They just continue with their daily routines, you know why? They are sure there is water, knowing they never left any of their water bills unpaid. When they insert their electronic cards into the ATM machines, they just punch in the amount they want to withdraw, because they know how much credit is available in their accounts. Why don't they practice the same faith where it concerns the things of *God?*

You have faith that *God* can heal a headache, stomachache, cold or flu, but you struggle to believe when it comes to HIV, cancer and other life-threatening diseases. Your faith carries as far as a headache, whenever it's cancer or HIV, you lock your Bible inside the closet, where your faith automatically runs dry. A problem experienced by most Christians; they measure their faith by visible things, and the importance of those things.

I love *Apostle Paul* very much, because he understood, by applying only his own faith, he wasn't going to achieve anything, that's why he wrote: *'For through the law I died to the law that I might live for God. I have been crucified with Christ, it is no longer I who live, but Christ who lives in me, and the life I now live in the flesh I live by faith in the Son of God, who loved me and gave Himself up for me.' (Galatians 2:20 &21)*

Paul understood that for him to achieve in *God's* business, he had to live by faith in *Jesus Christ*. The problem is that you live by your own faith, instead of living by faith through *Jesus*. To tell the truth, your own faith is going to fail, whereas *God's* faith is going to move mountains on your behalf. I remember once in my teenage years, I was faced with a tough and austere situation, whereby I lost my own beloved sister. At the same time I experienced rejection, chased away from home by my stepparents. I cursed *God* for all those happenings, for I thought He had forsaken me. I went into a series of prayer and fasting whilst living on the streets, and *God* revealed His secrets unto me.

I would have been unable to function at *God's* junction while my sister was still around, because I became too busy, to pay attention to *God*. I nursed my sister, her life was riddled with illness. I didn't have time to pray or read the Bible, until *God* did His will, in order to get my attention. When *God* is ready to use you, to take you to another level, to turn your life around, He takes away, that which you hold dear and love most. It could be your family, job, husband, wife or business. He considers how much it's worth to you; even so He wants you to place Him first in your life, above anything or anyone. Some of you are not suffering due to anything you did. *God* wants your attention. You have become too busy, to make time for *God*. Your full attention is focused on your job, child, wife, boyfriend, car or business, forgetting that those things were given to you by *God*. Christians have a big problem, whenever *God* bless them, they have a tendency to misuse or abuse those blessings. You're suffering because you want to be related to the blessing, rather than the Blesser. Don't you know that *God* gives and also takes away?

While the Israelites were still in the desert, *God* stopped manna to fall from heaven. He wanted the people's attention, for they were about to enter into the Promised Land. *God* stopped manna in order to retain their attention to the purpose He had for them.

As a Child of God, don't become conformed to the things of this world, yes you live in it, but you're not of it. When you face adversity, picture it as an advantage. Remember how *Isaac* prospered in the midst of harsh economic conditions. In a time of famine the Bible says he prospered. He became so prosperous, the Philistines ended up envying him. *(Genesis 26: 14)*

Your prosperity should be born out of the Word of *God,* despite of circumstances. You mustn't be perturbed by the high rates of inflation. When prices rise, don't complain, cry or feel bad. I know if I tell you it will be to your own advantage, you will think I am crazy. Your question will be: "How could it be, since my money won't be able to buy anything?" Well, as a Child of God, let your mind soar beyond the prevailing economic problems surrounding you. Don't think about how big your problem is rather think how big your God is. Think about the whole universe as yours, for indeed it's yours. *'Therefore let no one boast in man. For all things are yours' (1 Corinthians 3:21).*

Even if you run a small tuck-shop beyond that little corner on a particular street, you can still succeed in that little corner. Have a victory mentality, that wherever you are, that's where *God* also is. There is a hidden treasure in the land where you are, in spite of the tough austere situations. You can still progress and be a success, even if the whole world is struggling under a recession. You only have to see your problems as projects! *Isaac* when he was faced with the problem of famine, he turned it into a project, by putting his seed down, when everyone else was busy complaining and grumbling. And indeed it became a project, because the Bible says that he reaped a hundredfold, isn't that a miracle in times of famine?! *(Genesis 26:12-14)*

Beloved brethren it's never too late. You can still turn your problems into projects, in spite of your circumstances you can progress in abundance, grow until you become very rich. *If God is for us, who can be against us? (Romans 8:31)* God greatly blessed *Obed-Edom* the Gittite, and his household, because he accepted the ark of *God* wholeheartedly. *(2 Samuel 6:12)*

King David was afraid to take the ark of *God* with him, due to what he and the Israelites witnessed. *Uzzah* tried to take hold of the ark when the oxen stumbled. *God* put him to death immediately, because of his irreverent act. *(2 Samuel 6:6-9) Obed-Edom*, one who didn't even know how to pray, was greatly blessed because he received *God's* ark not as a problem, but as a project! *(2 Samuel 6:10 & 11)*

In all your sufferings there is a glory to be revealed, never ever think *God* has forsaken you. The world will reject you, but *God* will always love you unconditionally. *I consider the sufferings for this present time, not worth comparing with the glory that is to be revealed in us. Creation waits with eager longing for the revealing of the sons of God. (Romans 8: 18-19)* Problems could be lasting but they're not everlasting, *thus we have been made more than conquerors,* because we trust in God! *(Romans 8: 37).* As Children of God we should learn to develop and soar above things, even with loads and loads of troubles, trials and tribulations, all you need to know, is that you will not remain in the same situation, as long as you acknowledge *God.* Just like seasons they come and go. We cannot change them to our own liking, because that's the way *God* planned it, and it has to be. We as Children of *God* are on a journey towards the 'Promised Land,' like the Israelites. During this journey we will meet different perils and similarly we have to find ways to deal with it, why? For we have been given the Spirit of *God*, the spirit of faith, hope and the greatest of all love. The Bible is our road map. In this world we will suffer problems that cause pain emotionally, spiritually and physically.

Failure to deal with these problems leads to stress, depression and despair. The manner in which we handle our problems, are a clear indication of our spiritual maturity. Sometimes we face tough situations that may be overriding us, thus we need to be reminded of the living hope found in *Jesus Christ.*

(1 Corinthians 15:13). Unless the seed is buried underground, it will never germinate; Jesus was crucified and buried so that He would rise to victory for us. (John 12:24 & 1 Corinthians 15:57)

Therefore at times, struggles are exactly what we need in our lives. If we were to go through life without any obstacles, it would cripple us. We would not be as strong as we could be. I am certain that troubles actually make us strong. If I had not endured hardships, I would not have been here today. We should learn to turn every stumbling block that comes our way into a stepping stone, because we are more than conquerors! Whatever situations we may encounter in life, we need to remember we have living hope, found in *Jesus Christ!*

CHAPTER 2

PRAYING FOR YOURSELF

Then Hezekiah turned his face to the wall, and prayed to the Lord and said ``Remember me, O Lord, I have walked before You in truth and with a loyal heart, and have done what is good in Your sight." (Isaiah 38:2)

Hezekiah understood that he had sinned and fallen short of the glory of *God,* thus he decided to kneel down and pray. As king he could call or summon any great prophet besides *Isaiah* to come and pray for him. However, he decided to pray himself, why? He realised that it was now his own fish to fry; it was between him and *God* alone. It was not a man who announced that failure has overcome him; but *God,* therefore he had to set his house in order, for he surely was going to die. Even though it was *Isaiah* who spoke to *Hezekiah* he was sent by *God* Himself, in other words *God* used *Isaiah* as His mouthpiece. *(2 Kings 18-20)*

It's your priestly ministry as a believer to pray for yourself. You're to pray for the impact of *God's* Word to increase in your life. Whenever the impact of God's Word increases in your life, it creates room for prosperity.

The challenge nowadays is, the world is filled with a bunch of lazy Christians who grew used to being laid hands on, by certain men of *God.* What do the prophets or pastors possess, that are driving you to queue and waste your money, just so they could foretell you your future? Aren't prophets and pastors human beings like everyone else? Do they not eat, sleep, cry, and feel pain or pass through sufferings, like all of us?

Many Christians today have a wrong interpretation concerning the Word of God, that's why today there are too many fetish priests and prophets. Even though, most people are not to blame, they fail to pray, due to the so- called doctrines that are dismantling the Word of God inside most Christians. They teach that it is only the bishops, priests, pastors, prophets, evangelists who may pray, but the Bible does not confirm this. Note: Anything that is not Scripture is either satanic or carnal. Gone are the days of manna, approaching are times whereby men have to work and sweat before they could satisfy their fleshly needs. The issue is that you want your problems to be everybody's, forgetting that even prophets have their own problems they need to attend to. When will they get time to attend to their own problems, when they are busy carrying your burdens day and night? You must break out of that anti-Christ syndrome, depending on prophets to move mountains on your behalf.

When you're faced by a challenge, it is your challenge, instead of grumbling and complaining, kneel down and pray. You have faith that *God* can hear the prophets, but you doubt that He can hear your own prayer. You are afraid to pray for yourself, because you know that the ground you're standing on is not 'holy ground.' I don't mean standing literally, but what is your position in *God*? To put this plainly, is your relationship with *God* a straight forward one?

I remember when I was a little boy I couldn't enter my stepdad's presence if I did something wrong. Instead, I sent my younger sister to speak on my behalf, as my relationship with my stepdad was not good. I counted and saw myself unworthy to stand in his presence. It's similar to most Christians today. They can't face *God,* for they know their deeds do not please Him. They assume that when they pray, *God* is going to question them about their evil deeds.

God doesn't judge you on your past. He cares about what you do daily. Therefore *God* hands you a clean sheet of paper everyday of your life. When you mess up, and the writing consists out of lies, gossiping, stealing and fornicating, He takes that sheet and throws it into the fire, and forgets about it. When your sheet is filled with writings on truth, respect, love, offerings in church, tithes and helping the underprivileged, *God* keeps that sheet of paper as your legacy. Now, whenever you start confessing your sins in prayer, *God* is surprised, because His records do not outline all those things you are confessing. Instead of confessing so much junk, rather worship *God for* His love and greatness. *God* is just and fair; He forgives and forgets once and for all. Do you know why? There is nothing you did, or you're going to do that He doesn't know about.

"Before I formed you in the womb I knew you, before you were born I sanctified you; I ordained you a prophet to the nations." (Jeremiah 1:5) God knew everything about you, even before the foundation of the world. He knew you were going to steal, lie fornicate, commit adultery, murder, but He still ordained you. There is nothing you are going to do that is going to make *God's* love for you deteriorate, and nothing that is going to make Him love you more.

God already loves you more than enough. He died for you through His Son, *Jesus* by allowing Him to be crucified on the Cross, to pay for your and my sins. He became poor for you to be rich, suffered so you and I could receive joy and gladness. He allowed the crowd and Roman soldiers to spit on Him, that you and I could receive redemption through His anguish. *Jesus* bought you at a high price. Every problem you are faced with, you're supposed to lie down before God, and face Him in prayer. Instead, you start recalling your past mistakes, your family background and all your wrong doings. You begin to value yourself unworthy to stand before the presence of *God*. You must break with that stupid syndrome! The Bible states: *'Therefore, if anyone is in Christ, he is a new creation; old things have passed away; behold all things have become new.' (2 Corinthians 5:17)* Background doesn't mean your back is on the ground, it's simply information on where you come from, not where you are, or going.

God is not worried about where you're coming from; He is interested in where you're going. *God* didn't allow *Moses* to see His face but allowed him to see His back, you know why? Scripture teaches us that no man can see *God* and live, for His glory is too much to behold. *(Exodus 33:20-23)* In *2 Chronicles 7:14* God wants us to seek His face, do you know why? He longs for us to enter His presence. He wants us to stand in close relationship with Him. We know from the Bible that *God* always existed, and that He will always exist. Stop grumbling and complaining about your past, focus on your future. *God* has good plans for all of us. *Jeremiah 29:11-13- ''For I know the plans I have for you," declares the Lord, "plans to prosper you and not to harm you, plans to give you hope and a future. Then you will call upon Me and come and pray to Me, and I will listen to you. You will seek Me and find Me, when you seek Me with all your heart."*

There is a place that *God* wants you to reach and you can never reach that place when you still suffer from 'the background syndrome.' You can never tap into your blessings if you still clinging to your past, and simultaneously feel afraid to face *God*. The thing causing you to fail to pray for yourself is your lack of insight. You lack vision. When you lack vision, similarly your future seems insecure. *VISION + PRAYER = SECURE FUTURE*, without vision it is impossible to function at *God's* junction. Write down your vision and lay it plain on the tables.

Here follows prove that praying for yourself is your priestly ministry: Our *Lord Jesus* prayed for Himself. He could have asked the priests or pharisees to pray for Him, but He understood that it was His own mountain, only He could make that mountain move. As a Child of *God*, understand that you are unique and distinct. We are created to accomplish something that no one else can. You're very necessary, in order to pray for yourself! You're a Child of *God*. You are born to manifest the glory of *God* inside you. *God's* glory is not only in pastors and prophets, it's in everyone.

Most people think that a great *God* will descend from the sky and take away all suffering and pain. They forget that *God* put us in charge of the universe. He gave us dominion over all things, to rule and subdue. *(Genesis 1:28)* Then why are problems / challenges depicting the story of your life? Why is poverty, sickness, unemployment, barrenness, lack of money and all other austere situations causing you to be cast down? Why do problems dominate the next step of your life?

I think that if all the wild animals would migrate from the wild and take over our homes, we would migrate and reside where they were residing! Instead of us having dominion over them, they scare us, and I tend to ask:"Which is wiser man or beast?"

Witches and wizards will then be enabled to take a rightful stand in not worshipping our *God*, for materialistically they have much more than we, the Children of *God*. How are you going to explain to and convince worldly people that *God* is great, when you cry and complain more than them? Instead of them coming to you, you are the one that goes to them to borrow money, ask for help and even to be laid hands on. Haven't you heard what *God* plans for us? *(Jeremiah 29:11) God* wants us to be the most satisfied people in the universe. *'Behold, I will send you grain and new wine and oil; and you will be satisfied by them. I will no longer make you a reproach among the nations.' (Joel 2:19)*

Christians are the people who are supposed to take the lead in technology, business, and finance. In all areas we should get the first fruits. Worldly people must long to worship *God Almighty,* because they notice the extraordinary way in which *God* bless us in our everyday lives.

We will win souls for the Kingdom of Heaven, sometimes without uttering even a single word, but through the example of our lifestyle. For the best Gospel is not the one we read or preach, but the one we live. So I urge you brethren in *Christ,* learn to pray for yourselves. The fact that you are unable to pray for yourselves, are actually making you a reproach amongst the heathens. You're making it easy for them to formulate a theory that suggests and advocates that *Jesus Christ* is a lie.

Many religions advocate *Jesus Christ* never existed. They theorise the whole story, assuming it was only a white man's strategy devised, in order to colonise the black nation. But, as Children of *God* we are witnesses that *Jesus* is real. He lives. We saw, and still see His hands perform miracles and wonders in our lives. You are supposed to move your own mountain. *God* cannot do anything, when you are doing nothing! For *God* to move, you must initiate the first step, and *God* will take ten steps at once towards you. Your problem is, you only pray once, and wrongly assume the battle is won. Do you not know that there are spiritual powers that fight your prayers, trying to prevent them from reaching the ear of *God?* *Daniel* prayed, but only received his answer after twenty-one days. *God* heard his prayer the first day he prayed. *God* answered him the very first day. *However,* his answer got delayed for twenty-one days, because the devil was fighting, trying to prevent the answer from reaching *Daniel*.

'And he said to me, "O Daniel, man greatly beloved, understand the words that I speak to you, and stand upright, for I have now been sent to you." While he was speaking these words to me, I stood trembling. Then he said to me, "Do not fear, Daniel, for from the first day that you set your heart to understand, and to humble yourself before your God, your words were heard; and I have come because of your words. "But the prince of the kingdom of Persia withstood me twenty-one days; and behold, Michael one of the chief princes, came to help me, for I had been left alone there with the king of Persia."'(Daniel 10:11-13)

Understand that whenever you pray, your answer could come after a week, month, year or decade, depending on the severity of the battle taking place in the spiritual realm. That is why you must pray without ceasing. Pray for yourself. Don't ask pastors, prophets or bishops, do it yourself. You are the answer to your problems. No one is better equipped than you to pray for you! Your life is in *God's* hands, but it is also in your hands, for you are the one living your life. Your attitude will always determine your altitude. The depth of any foundation determines the height of the building, likewise the depth of your faith determines the quantity of your blessing. Don't measure your faith by visible things, but things yet to come!

CHAPTER 3

SPEAK POSITIVELY ABOUT YOURSELF

'The mouth of the righteous is a well of life, but violence covers the mouth of the wicked.' (Proverbs 10:11)

'In the mouth of a fool is a rod of pride, but the lips of the wise will preserve' (Proverbs 14:3)

If you want yourself to progress to the next level, speak positively about yourself at all times. Many don't realise it, but damaging words cause more destruction than physical weapons. Most Christians are more often broken down by unguarded and damaging utterances from either themselves or by those they lead or either by those who lead them, than by physical weapons of the devil.

Mark 11:23 Jesus teaches on the importance of and power in words when He says:*"You shall have what you say."* Thus, the positive words you speak about yourself will enhance your peace, progress, and success. It parallels in a sense the words of the *Apostle Paul* in **Ephesians 4:29: "Let no corrupt word proceed out of your mouth, but what is good for necessary edification."** Corrupt communication is any utterance, word, speech or question that destroys rather than builds up. Let the words you speak about yourself, be words that will shape, build up, prosper, grow you spiritually and teach others to do likewise.

Remember, you are a Child of *God* therefore your words are loaded with power. *(Ecclesiastes 8:4)* Don't curse, rather bless. Always speak positively about yourself. Most Christians are very quick and good at blaming the devil, evil spirits, demons, witches and wizards when faced with austere times. Why don't you trace back your steps, and find the root of the problem? After all, no one has ever seen the devil, but all of us heard about him! It is you who bewitched yourself by the negative words that proceeded out of your mouth. Every time you face a challenge or predicament, you start devaluating yourself, resulting in breaking down your self-esteem, destroying your self-confidence. You meditate on why things in your marriage, job, car, home, business, education are not going well. It lies in the way you speak about those things. I perceived married couples, and how they converse doesn't exhibit a single drop of love between them. Married couples are supposed to do things together, for they are one.

'Therefore shall a man leave his father and his mother and be joined to his wife, and they shall become one flesh.' (Genesis 2:24)

Being one flesh simply means having one mind, but in today's marriages the husband wants this and the wife wants that, that's why so many marriages don't last long. Even if you're married to a bad partner, the best thing to do is to prophesy positively over them all the time. *Proverbs 23:7: 'As a man thinketh, so is he.'* So whenever you speak positively about your bad partners, *God* is changing their situation, to correspond with the words you proclaiming about, and over them.

Even in your business, when there is no profit growth, and your business stands on the brink of bankruptcy or liquidation, prophesy that your business is booming, successful and very profitable. As long as you say it with faith, you shall have what you say. In other words, your success lies in what proceeds out of your mouth. If it is bad, then know that everything about your life will fall apart and break into pieces. But, if it is good, *God* guarantees you overflowing blessings.

In your sphere of contact you are labeled bad and aggressive names, because of the negative way you speak about yourself. When you're in trouble you shrink and evaluate yourself as nobody. You are experiencing a 'dry' season. It doesn't define you as a person.

Since the day I started speaking, I never spoke negative about myself. Even though I had nothing, not even a roof over my head. I prophesied over myself that I was an influential, rich, powerful man. Guess what *God* did? He made me always be amongst influential and wealthy people. I couldn't abide among poor people who had nothing, like me, because my mindset was different from theirs.

The challenge may lie inside your marriage, business, job, home or health. All these levels seem 'dry' and 'dead.' Instead of prophesying positively over those circumstances, you speak damaging words which curse your life, making your situation worse, than it already is.

Satan doesn't want you to succeed or progress in anything. He doesn't enter your life uninvited. He waits and seeks someone to devour. The very moment you tell yourself you can never make it, that you are down and out; the devil automatically seizes this golden opportunity to enter your life. It makes him happy when you confess poverty, sickness, suffering, unemployment, divorce and pain. Confessions like these make him feel great about his kingdom. Remember, through all your complaining you are exalting his kingdom, by glorifying his works. Negative or pessimistic words actually glorify the works of *Satan.* Your problems grow worse day by day. Simply put: The Kingdom of Hell rejoices over your pain and sufferings. By blaming the devil, you actually buying his story, that's what he and his angels of darkness are waiting for.

The devil doesn't want you to blame anyone else other than him, for he is the father of all problems and deceit! **(John 8:44)**

What is amazing is that he stands before the presence of *God* and mocks you, you know why? You give Satan undue credit by shifting all blame onto him. This is where he begins to value himself powerful, feeling all puffed up to the extent that he starts boasting. Often your suffering is a result of your unwise language. As a Child of *God* refuse: poverty, sickness, barrenness, unemployment and brokenness or to be cast down. Speak and prophesy good things over yourself. It is you, and only you who could change your image in society. Other people can never identify you with wealth, when you don't even confess being rich. The bad labels they hanged around your neck, only you alone could persuade them to change into positive, good labels. You possess power within you to turn this negativity into something positive and good.

Whenever you are weak confess that you are strong, when sick confess that you are healed, when attacked by poverty, tell yourself that you're far exceedingly richer than anyone in the world! Due to your confessions *God* will turn your life around in a miraculous way, even the people around you will be greatly amazed. If you want your life to be praise on earth, speak the kind of words prescribed in ***Deuteronomy 28:13:'And the Lord will make you the head and not the tail; you shall be above only, and not be beneath, if you heed the commandments of the Lord your God, which I command you today, and are careful to observe them.'***

It is a biblical principle: You must speak positively about yourself at all times.

The result of your blessing is going to positively change not only your life, but also the sphere of your contact. *God* wants you to be praise on earth. Whenever the heathens glance at you, they will crave to enter into the house of the *Lord,* because of the signs and wonders marking your life. *God* wants the Christians to be the most satisfied in the whole universe, not to be a reproach that is going to drive the heathens to question *God's* existence. It is written: *'Why should they say amongst the peoples,: "Where is their God?" Then the Lord became jealous for His land and had pity on His people. The Lord answered and said to His people: "Behold I will send you grain and new wine and oil, and you will be satisfied and I will no longer make you a reproach among nations."' (Joel 2: 17-19)* Being satisfied doesn't only mean having plenty, it means having more than enough.

Good people of *God*; understand that *God* wants to grant you the dew of the morning, which I refer to as the first blessing. *God* wants you to be an ultimate praise on earth. When David says*:"I have been young, and now am old, yet have I not seen the righteous forsaken, nor his descendants begging for bread". (Psalm 37:25) David* was not advocating that Christians will never suffer, or face austere times. He was simply painting a picture, although the righteous could be faced with poverty, sickness, pain, suffering, unemployment, barrenness, financial instability and all other known problems, they don't panic and run around complaining like the people of the world. Instead, they turn those adversities into advantages, because their words possess power to speak things into existence. They confess riches, blessed marriages, happy families, great jobs, blooming businesses, and *God* covers them with His blessings and favour, you know why? He doesn't want you to be a reproach among the heathens. *God* wants you to be the most satisfied people in the universe!

Your problems can never be transformed into projects if you still nurse that idle mentality. Be careful of whatever words proceed out of your mouth, it will be decisive regarding your progress or your downfall. Negative, pessimistic words are nothing but wind, and they blow unkind. In other words, whatever you speak about yourself, will always echo back unto you. Take caution therefore not to speak damaging words, for they will echo back into you, casting you down. When you speak positive, optimistic words your life shall always reflect greatness. You shall rise when everybody else is falling. *God* is ready to take you to another level. Are you ready to speak in accordance with His plan?

Are you ready to speak in line with what *God* has instore for you? The answer lies in your mouth and tongue, for *God* is not looking for a man after His blessing, but one after His heart. When you seek after the heart of *God,* whatever proceeds out of your mouth will be building up, shaping, mending, rebuilding and altering the universe, bringing praise to *God,* the Creator of the universe. *God* has created you to be a 'wow' factor, therefore surprise the world! *God's* grace and mercy will forever be the story of your life. You shall do extraordinary things in your lifetime!

CHAPTER 4

RE-ESTABLISH YOUR OWN WORLD

'By faith we understand that the world was framed by the word of God, so that things which are seen were not made out of things which are visible.' (Hebrews 11:3).

The reason why so many in the world today seem to have only the short end of the stick, living from hand to mouth, is due to ignorance, how to literally catapult themselves out of scarcity into abundance, by applying the principles revealed in *God's* Word. You can re-create your own world, and result a positive change in your profession, marriage, and finances – whatever it is, you can change it.

Isaiah 60:1: 'Arise, shine, for your light has come! And the glory of the Lord rises upon you.' Yes the light of God is upon you, but it is your duty to make it shine. In fact it's your rightful responsibility to result a change, even from glory to glory. How? With your words! The Bible says:".... *and this is the victory that over cometh the world, even our faith." (1John 5:4)*. You faith-filled declaration will create the realities you want to see in your life, as well as that of your loved ones. The law that stands firm in the realm of the Spirit is: *'He will have whatever he says.' (Mark 11:23)*

Consequently, the changes you seek are only a 'mouth-work' away. If you think the conditions of your life, your place of work, or at home are very tough and in a deplorable state, do as *God* did. *'In the beginning God created the heavens and the earth. Now the earth was without form, and void; and darkness was on the face of the deep. And the Spirit of God was hovering over the face of the waters. Then God said:" Let there be light;" and there was light.' (Genesis 1-3)* Re-create your own world with your words, speak forth and turn everything about your life around. The whole earth remained a dark mass until *God* spoke, when He spoke there was a turnaround of things. *Genesis 1:2-27.*

Most Christians fail to re-create their world, because they suffering from 'miracle syndrome.' They wait and hope while praying, that *God* is going to affect a change in their lives, on their behalf. They forget that the days of manna are passed. *God* granted you power to speak, your circumstances will turnaround after you spoken. Your problem is that you pray too much and act too little. You pray without understanding, that's why you continue to pray for things already belonging to you. You have faith, but your faith isn't accompanied by deeds. You believe, but don't take action. You forget that faith without deeds is dead. *(James 2:17)*. You even pray for things you're not supposed to pray for, not all situations are supposed to be prayed for. There are some situations you must pray over, and others you must speak to. The Bible states:*"And He arose and rebuked the wind, and said to the sea, "Peace, be still!" And the wind ceased, and there was a great calm" (Mark 4:39)*

Jesus led by example. If the disciples were left on their own, they would have prayed and spoke in tongues all the time. *Jesus* only spoke a few words and there was a great turnaround of things. That's why the Bible says that we must speak as kings and pray as priests. Why? Kings possess power and authority to affect any change they want, whenever they feel like it. *(Proverbs 16:10 &*
1 Peter 2:5)

As a Child of *God,* you have been placed as king in the place where you are, in order to speak, and move mountains at the sound of your voice. Command your problems to convert into projects, if you want your world to be re-created. You can never move mountains, when you speak like a slave. Slaves do not think for themselves, their masters do. They cannot command or introduce anything new, you know why? They don't possess power or authority to do so. Whatever they say, is always considered last.

The turnaround of your world is being determined by the power of your words. To re-create your world you must be amazingly eloquent in speech.

Apostle Paul, when he was still *Saul*, could arrest the whole church with just a handwritten piece of paper. Even you could be enabled to overcome the most austere conditions in your life, by just uttering one or two words eloquently. The problem seems to be, that the Church today is fully packed with a bunch of lazy and weak Christians, who expect *God* to fight the devil on their behalf. Be careful not to be counted as one of them, otherwise your life will always be synonymous with poverty, sickness, suffering, unemployment, barrenness, financial instability and of course permanent downfall.

Never allow your life to be controlled by the economy, that is: inflation, recession, job scarcity, medical scarcity and basic commodity shortage, but let your life be controlled by the words that proceed out of your mouth. The problem is that you became so used to the Word of *God*, so used to His grace, His unmerited favour He bestows upon you. You became so used to attending church, that's why you can take a day off, staying home doing nothing. Others may sleep in and drink black coffee in bed, when they supposed to be in the house of *God*. You pray whenever you feel like praying, fast whenever your thoughts hit the word fasting.

Good weather Christians really exist! When it's cold or raining they would rather stay at home, than get wet for the glory of *God*. Others file and sign up for overtime, you know why? They became so comfortable being busy with the things of *God*; they end up forgetting who *God* is. He is not just *God*, but the One who created every visible thing in the universe. The King of kings! The Conquering Lion of the twelve tribes of Judah! The

Ancient of all Days, the One who is never too early neither too late, but is always right inside *God's* timing. He is so high no one can go over Him, so low no one can go under Him and so wide, no one can go around Him. His name is *Jehovah*, for He is the *Most High God*! If you want to re-establish you world, never become too used to the things of *God*, but fear the *Lord* your *God*.

As *God* created the world, I want you to know that the same can happen in your life, however only, when you speak the right words. Develop a mental picture and begin to incubate upon the changes you want in your life, as well as in the sphere of your contact. You cannot re-create your world if you still cling to that victim mentality inside you. You must evict that mentality of ungodliness; otherwise you might never be able to function at *God's* junction.

The big issue is that you are living with a victim mentality. You are so focused on what you went through, complaining about how unfair it was; not realising you are dragging the pains of the past into your present and future. It's almost as though you get up each day and fill a big wheelbarrow with junk from the past, and bring it into the new day. Let go of your past and all the things you have been through. There is no need for your past to poison your future. Just because you've been through some hurt and pain, or perhaps one or more of your dreams were shattered, doesn't mean *God* doesn't have another plan for your life. *God* still has a bright future instore for you. However, you must understand this principle: 'The past is the past.' Your attitude should be: "I refuse to dwell on the negative things that happened to me. I am not going to think about all I have lost. I am not going to focus on what could or should have been mine, no. I am going to draw the line in the sand. This is a new beginning, and I am moving forward, knowing that *God* has a bright future instore for me." If you change your attitude and speak the above words over your life, *God* will give you all the desires of your heart, thus will enable you to re-establish your own world.

Quit mourning over things already over and done with. You have to shake off that victim mentality inside you, and start having a 'victor' mentality. Meditate on what *God* said in His Word about your problem or situation. Within a short period of time you will receive the inspired Word filled with power, which when put into practice, changes things. That's the weapon you must use to re-create your world. *God's* Word in your mouth is the power you need, it's the same Word that created and still upholds the universe. Put that power into practice today, speak a Word of Faith and re-create your world! Yesterday is not yours to recover, but tomorrow is yours to win or lose. If you truly want to re-create your own world, you must be grounded in the Word of *God.* Your life must be covered with the Words that *God* spoke. Know the promises that *God* speaks over, and into your life. When you start speaking, you will not speak in vain, but you shall repeat what the Father and the Son spoke, and what the Holy Spirit is speaking today.

You will see tremendous results in your life, not coming to pass by fire or force, but by *God's Spirit (Zechariah 4:6)*. You shall start defeating those things that always defeated you. Re-creating your own world, needs you to be steadfast in doing what is right in the eyes of *God*. You must live righteousness, then whatever you say, you will have. Remember, *God* is not a respecter of a person, but of His principles, therefore He will never go against His Word. When He says you shall prosper, indeed you shall prosper. When He says you shall be rich, indeed you shall be rich, in fact all the promises He spoke about you shall come to pass, as long as you abide in Him and His Word abides in you!

In conclusion, the Bible says: *"You will say to this mountain move, and it will move". (Matthew 17:20 & 21)* I tell you also, you shall speak unto the world of poverty, pain, sickness, suffering, unemployment, barrenness, and all upheavals be re-created, and it shall be as you have spoken. The only principle is that you must be in right standing with *God*, for your words to have power and evoke change. Without righteousness it is impossible to re-create your own world!

CHAPTER 5

REJECT POVERTY

'The rich man's world is his strong city; the destruction of the poor is their poverty.' (Proverbs 10:15)

Many today are sinking into the thralldom of poverty, because they allowed socio- economic upheavals present in today's world, to determine their state of mind as well as their lifestyle. If you are born-again it doesn't matter what is conspiring around you, refuse to be poor. If you are a Christian, the truth in *God's* Word, is that all wealth in the universe belongs to you. The Bible states that even *Jesus* grew up poor, so that He can have empathy with us, and the situations we face. Whenever we pray about our situations, speaking *God's* Word into our situations, we can receive whatever we ask, as long as we pray and speak *God's* will. Therefore, if we need finances, *God* will provide in our need. We don't need to go through life poor, we can be rich. We only need to change our mentality from victim to victor, and our words from negative to positive, and our prayers need to be filled with faith, then we can receive what we ask for. The Bible states: *James 4:2 & 3: You do not have, because you do not ask God. When you ask, you do not receive, because you ask with wrong motives.*"

'For you know the grace of our Lord Jesus Christ, that though He was rich, for your sakes He became poor that through His poverty you might become rich.'(2 Corinthians 8:9)

He took upon Himself not only the sins of the world, but also the after effects of sin, one which is poverty. You must refuse poverty. Poverty is a result of poor human mentality, which originates in the mind. If your mind always thinks negative things, you will reap what you sow, and unfortunately it will be nothing other than failure. *God* is rich. How can you serve Him and remain poor? He didn't say that the street of heaven is coated with gold instead, made out of gold. Gold and silver belong to Him. (*Revelation 21:21 & Haggai 2:8)*

As a Child of *God* you are an heir of the Kingdom of *God,* you hold a rightful passport to the riches and treasures of heaven. Thus, economic necessity must not cast you down and make you identify with poverty. Wherever you are, *God* has tailor-made you to be in that place to advertise Him. When you are poor, then how is the character of *God* going to be seen in you by the worldly people? *God's* promise to bless *Abraham* wasn't to *Abraham* alone but to his seed after him. Understand that the seed referred to in the Bible isn't *Isaac, Abraham's* physical descendant, but to *Christ,* and the Bible says: *'Now if we are children, then heirs- heirs of God and joint heirs with Christ, if indeed that we suffer with Him, that we may be also glorified together.' (Romans 8:17)*

As long as you are a Child of *God,* then you are a joint heir with *Jesus Christ.* Thus, to place more emphasis, you are the possessor of all things. Everything that belongs to *Christ* belongs to you. The problem is that our present universe is fully packed with 'manna syndrome' people. You want *God* to do miracles on your behalf. But *Jesus* never stated that He was going to do miracles for us while in ever beautiful heaven, but He stated that we are to perform more miracles than Him. *'And Jesus said unto them, "Because of your unbelief; for assuredly, I say to you, if you have faith as a mustard seed, you will say to this mountain, 'Move from here to there,' and it will move; and nothing will be impossible for you.' "(Matthew 17:20).*

Jesus didn't say that He would speak. He said that we ourselves as long as we do things in faith, nothing shall ever be impossible for us. You are failing to receive your blessings because of your attitude. Your attitude determines what you will be, poor or rich. Everybody wants to be identified with greatness, even so, when *Jesus* was given the privilege to be great, He humbled Himself. *God* gave you a 'penalty kick' in life, but you missed it, because of your attitude. You cannot put on an attitude and take it off again. Is *Christ* in you or on you?

Some people are spiritually 'asleep,' but even so *God* brought good things unto them. Unfortunately they are unable to receive these good things, due to them being 'asleep.' You received

Christ inside you. However, His power is lying dormant inside you, waiting for you to awake. Before you don't wake up, your life will never shine. You are failing to rebuke the storm, to stop the rain, simply because you don't realise that *Christ's* power is inside you, or if He isn't, it is time you get saved, so that you can receive *Christ* inside you, and start moving in His power.

The only reason why *Jesus* decided to sleep in the back of the boat was because He tested the level of faith of His disciples. Were their faith matured enough to enable them to take care of themselves in the midst of the storm? He is the Beginning and the End. He knew the storm was going to rage, even so He decided to sleep. *Jesus* knew the storm was nothing to be afraid of. Unfortunately the disciples grew scared and decided to wake Him up, even though they were the ones faced with the storm, not *Jesus*. He was sleeping in the lower deck. *(Mark 4:35-39)*

You are really good at being a Christian on the inside, not so on the outside. On the outside you're empty and poor. When *Christ* is inside you, you will not panic when faced with austere situations. You will stand your ground and face the enemy bravely. You would be bold enough to fight the devil. Once you realise that *Christ* is inside you, you will start using His power and authority in your austere situations.

In this world we are at war, for where there is no war there can never be a victory. You must plead with *God* to arise in your circumstances, and give you a turnaround breakthrough. Every serpent of destruction working against your destiny must be put to death through the mighty Name of *Jesus*. You must be prepared to engage in warring prayers. You need to pull down every stronghold against you, every imaginary thing and anything else that wants to exalt itself against the knowledge of *God*. All sufferings *Satan* put you through in life, all fears, mental or physical torture, all hatred, poverty, misfortune, and hindrances also all evil works of *Satan*.

All these things cause you to feel intimidated by your own fears, and you end up accepting poverty. Any 'spiritual screen' the devil uses to monitor your progress, any 'spiritual mirror,' and tape recorded speech, cameras which the devil set up against you, must be destroyed in *Jesus* Name. You could be enabled to do so, when in your natural state, you allow the supernatural *(God)* to intertwine with your natural state, for you to start functioning in a 'supernatural' way. It is written: *'The key of the house of David I will lay on his shoulders; so he shall open, and no one shall shut, and he shall shut and no one shall open.' (Isaiah 22:22)*

You are now faced with poverty, the whole world let you down, there is nowhere for you to go. You tried to accumulate riches in a world full of hatred, but I know that you could carry on. The moment you start confessing you're rich and not poor, you obtain a certain level of spiritual maturity, and operate from that place. You are poor because a certain door was opened to you, or you entered a doorway you were not supposed to enter. Fortunately *God* handed *Jesus* the keys to the Kingdom of Heaven, and He is going to shut the door of poverty in your life once and for all, and no power would be able to reopen that door, ever again! He is going to open the door to prosperity, riches, success and a satisfied robust life, and none shall be able to close that door, not now, not ever.

The *Lord* shall increase you more and more - you and your children. According to the book of (***Deuteronomy 28:1-13)*** you have been destined to be a winner, not a loser, a blessing not a curse, the head not the tail, the first not the last, to be above not beneath. *'The blessing of the Lord makes one rich, and He adds no sorrow with it.' (Proverbs 10:22)* You are created for signs and wonders. Miracles should happen in every corner of your life, as it's written:*"Here I am and the children whom the Lord has given me! We are signs and symbols in Israel; from the Lord of Hosts, who dwells on Mount Zion (Isaiah 8:18)*

Whatever conspires in your life, your life lies in your hands, only you have the power to refuse poverty. All *God's* promises made to *Abraham,* through whom he became possessor of all things, are fulfilled in you. No wonder *Paul* says that all things are yours. *(1 Corinthians 3:21)*

Let this become your mindset, for it is *God's* desire for you to be satisfied in all the spheres of your life! I have seen many Christians suffering so much, they end up asking for help from worldly people. Worldly people start making you a laughing stock, because when you go to them for help, you cannot preach the Good News to them, for it failed bringing any fruits unto your own life. Your relatives who are not Christians pity you. When you go to them seeking help, they start preaching to you about their own gods, how they benefit from them. When they hand you money, they don't forget to inform you, that it is sprinkled with ancestral concussions. Due to your desperation, you accept their money, and even show gratitude, not realising you said 'yes' to poverty. Poverty is not what *God* plans for your life. Listen what He says:*"Let the priests, who minister before the Lord, weep between the porch and the altar; let them say, 'Spare your people, O Lord and do not give your heritage to reproach, that the nations should rule over them. Why should they say among the peoples, 'Where is their God?'" (Joel 2:17)*

When you are a poverty stricken Christian, you make the heathens question your *God*. You actually become a reproach amongst them. You must by all means decline poverty, if not, your life make people devalue *God*'s power. Your life might lead worldly people to confess that *God* doesn't exist at all. You give them more reason to continue 'dying' in idolatry, for they won't see any reason to become Christians. Why would they choose a life of suffering and hardship? They will rather stay sinners and continue prospering, than stoop so low by worshipping your *God*. Be very careful what message your life carries across. Your main duty as a Child of *God*, is exhibiting His love and character to the world. How then can the world believe that *God* is love, when all they see, are you crying day and night? This is what you must ask yourself:"What is *God's* plan for my life?"Let me tell you what He says: - *"Behold, I will send you grain and new wine and oil, and you will be satisfied by them; and I will no longer make you a reproach among the nations" (Joel 2:19).*

When you look closely, all the above products are always found in the palaces of kings, as it represents wealth. *God's* will for you is to be rich in such a manner, even the heathens will want to join forces with you. Why is that? It's a sign that you truly exhibit the character of *God*. Your life is a living testimony to those around you. Brethren, the time arrived, it is now! Now is the time to stop, and demystify life. Now is the time to stop enduring life, and start enjoying it. It's that simple – Say 'No' to poverty!

CHAPTER 6

LEAVE YOUR COMFORT ZONE

Most Christians are so comfortable in the place where they find themselves, but has it been tailor-made for you by *God?* When people receive a command from *God* to leave their comfort zone, they seem puzzled and have questions. Why must *God* remove you out of your comfort zone, and take you to an unknown place? *God* wants to take you out of that warm, comforting area, because He purposed that place to only be your training ground. *God* in fact isn't taking you out, but is actually graduating you to another level of life. You spent more than enough time at your training ground. You don't even possess a permanent residency. You can never run *God's* race laid out for you, if you are still attached to the place where you underwent training, the place where you are now. The only reason why most Christians in today's world are poor, they became too complacent with the little they have. They make themselves feel better by referring to it as a stable life; due to too much scientific knowledge.

As stated by *Sir Isaac Newton*: *"A body continues in its state of rest or uniform velocity unless acted upon by some external force".* Well *God* is that Force that is going to cause you to migrate and go to the place *God* foreordained for you. The Bible says: *"Get out of your country and your family, and from your father's house, to a land that I will show you" (Genesis 12:1).* *God* saw *Abraham's* inability to function at His junction, while He was still in his comfort zone.

God wants to take you out of your present comfort zone. It may be a good home, business, job, city or country. He didn't create that as your final destination. *God* realised that your comfort zone became very dear to you, thus He is causing that place to 'dry up.' In a similar way *God* caused Brook Cherith to dry up, because He noticed that *Elijah* became satisfied to daily survive on bird meat. *God* transferred him to a place where he ate bread and water / wine *(1 Kings 17:2-16).* Now wasn't that a better place? *God* can never use you while you are still in your comfort zone. Before He could use *Abraham, Abraham* had to leave his own country. *Joseph* had to first pass through jail. *Paul* was struck by blindness. *God* is going to move you out of your comfort zone, because He saw that you shall 'die' there.

When *God* is ready to use you, there is always pain involved. You are going to pass through things that will override you. Do not adapt to a system, for you don't know when it is going to change, but adapt to God's plan, because His words have power to bring forth change that will be to your advantage. Do not leave your comfort zone when you see other people leaving, leave when *God* commands you to. Your problem is that you don't involve *God* in all your decisions. Your choices are influenced by what you see with your naked eye.

Lot chose to go eastwards because the grass there looked greener, and there were plenty of water for his livestock. He was unaware that the place he chose was near Sodom and Gomorrah, and that *God* had already planned to destroy the two cities, because the residents were very wicked. He found himself in trouble, due to him making his choice based on material things. What if the things he saw were just for a limited period of time, only for that season?

Every time you make choices without involving *God,* there is bound to be trouble. When you move together with *God,* even the people around you will simultaneously be amazed and confused. They won't accept, and will fail to understand, how and why you have to leave. When *God* is ready to take you to another dimension, He could distance you from your family, relatives and close friends. He could actually take away everything that you grew used to and are fond of. The place where you find yourself is called your 'place of rest,' it is not your permanent residing area.

The place where you are finding yourself is your *'Gilgal'* –a stopover towards your destiny. Do not grow too attached to your 'place of rest.' Sooner or later *God* is going to cause you to move out of that 'resting' place. The problem with Christians, they love to build around their 'place of rest' assuming it's their final destination.

God placed you in a 'place of rest' to re-think your actions. Don't accept it when people tell you it's a good place to settle, for *God* wants to move you to another level. Most people 'die' in situations where they not supposed to be, because they allow what is outside to influence their inside. What is presently happening in your life is causing you to reason and incline about it, but also to get done with it. You fell in love with that person, once again you moved from one place to another, changed jobs, and *God* noticed that you been wandering around a lot, therefore He placed you where you are now, in order for you to rest.

Resting is a time of meditation. You cannot think when you still wandering around. There are certain habits that you need to shake off in order to reach your destiny. That 'shake off' could only be achieved at your *'Gilgal.'* *'Gilgal'* is a place where your shame is being removed. Shame differs from guilt and embarrassment. Guilt is something that eats at your conscience, whenever you do wrong, something inside you speaks. Embarrassment is what you feel after doing wrong. Guilt wants you to hide. Shame, on the other hand, speaks louder than anything. People will ask you why you worship God, as you're still suffering, resulting feelings of shame inside you. *God* wants to use His rod at your *'Gilgal'* to roll away your shame and bad habits. People pointing fingers at you, will become confused. Something must be removed from your life, sometimes you may not even know what it is.

'Removal time' is uncomfortable, because some of the things you are so attached to, you don't want to let go, for you love it, or them very much! Don't be so attached to the things of the world, be attached to *God*. You want to hold on to the things you love, even though *God* wants you to let go. You are holding on to small things, because you don't posses insight of the bigger things *God* has instore for you. *God* placed you where you are, to remove inconsistency, for *'Gilgal'* is a place of remembrance. You can fall anywhere, but never accept falling at your *'Gilgal.'* Every person is responsible for all the good within the scope of his abilities, (for no more, none can tell whose sphere is the largest).

Your comfort zone is the only barrier standing between you and your destiny. I remember how *God* caused me to move out of my comfort zone. I was so attached to home, not due to any material things, but because of my beloved sister. She was my only reason for staying. Guess what *God* did? He took my sister away from me, she passed away and I had no reason to stay at home any longer. This sad event pushed me towards the land which *God* promised me. Just after I migrated, *God* started using me so mightily that I couldn't understand what was taking place in my life. That's how I learnt that *'Gilgal'* is a training ground, after learning your lessons, you graduate to another level.

You are failing to move forward, because you are not attached to *God*. When you are attached to *God*, it is less painful to leave your comfort zone, because you are intimate with *God*. Intimacy in other words means 'close, private, personal relationship.' Just as a married couple has a private, personal and very close relationship, likewise you will be able to form a private, personal and close relationship with *God*. Whenever you are ready to form an intimate relationship with *God*, He too will form such a relationship with you.

In your life there must be an umbilical cord that adjoins you to *God*. Unlike the one that connects a mother and her baby, yours with *God* must never be cut. It should be an eternal cord, that no matter how prevailing the troubles of this world may become, you will refuse to give up, because you will know that *God* is with you. The main reason why most people do not want to leave their '*Gilgal*,' is that they relate easier to blessings, rather than the One who blesses. The biological umbilical cord can be cut; or rather it must be cut as soon as the mother gives birth.

As a Christian, you should understand that you are not like tinned goods kept on shelves, and have an expiry date. It is time for you to grow; it is time to pull up your socks and to re-tool, for you are now facing a new battle.

When you were still a baby Christian you acted in a very peculiar way, but now that you know *God* much better, throw the childish things away. *'When I was a child, I spoke as a child, I understood as a child, I thought as a child; but when I became a man, I put away childish things' (1 Corinthians 13:11).*

Jesus said to His disciples, ***"Let us cross-over to the other side" (Mark 4:35).***

In your marriage, business, family, finances and all other aspects of your life, it is time to crossover to the other side. You are suffering because you have spoken, or thought or reasoned out of turn. Forget about your position at home and background, for it happened. This could fittingly be called your '*Gilgal*,' but understand well that *'Gilgal'* is not your permanent residency. Instead, learn to manage your past, it has a tendency of repeating itself, and it wants to catch up with you. When it does, you won't like it.

Grown up Christians manage things, situations and people, for growth has deep roots. Those roots contain knowledge of how to manage your life, family, marriage, business and money. Take heed, growing is not easy. The roots go deeper, when you start to go deeper in *God*. You will meet with trials, tribulations and trouble, but you should continue pushing deeper if you serious about reaching your destiny! You will be faced with opposition, but rejoice for the Bible says: *'If God be for us, who can be against us'* (Romans 8:31).

Let us bear in mind that growing is good, even so, pruning still has to take place. While you are growing, *God* is pruning you. He will make you pass through some stages, wherein you shouldn't stop growing and excelling. *God* will cut off the wrong things in your life, those things you consider right. Therefore Children of God, leave your comfort zones now, or *God* is going to cause you to do so. If you are really prepared to turn your lives around and turn your problems into projects, the secret to reaching your destiny lies in aborting and migrating away from your comfort zone!

It may be nice and comfortable now, but sooner or later you will regret staying in your comfort zone for too long. You cannot pray for something temporary to become permanent. You will pray until you die and nothing will happen. You cannot pray for a white house to be red. You can roll on your tummy, cry, scream and speak in tongues, but until you stand up, buy red paint and paint that house red, you will die a laughing stock.

Brethren, there is a land that is flowing with milk and honey awaiting you to dwell in. You overstayed in '*Gilgal*' far too long, now is the time to proceed and move towards your Canaan!

CHAPTER 7

UNDERSTAND GOD'S TIMING

Jesus replied, "My time has not yet come" (John 2:4).
Therefore Jesus told them: "The right time for me has not yet
come" (John 7:6).

Everything in this world works inside a time frame and
revolves around time. It's better to spend more time with *God*
than people, for people can hurt and disappoint you. Once you
understand the importance of time, it becomes easier to invest
in what is vital for your life. If you are going to be extraordinary
on earth, you must start to understand timing. Many Christians
are shrinking in the thralldom of poverty, finding themselves
unable to convert their problems into projects. They do not
understand the concept of *God's* timing. They think their timing
works similar to God's timing, not so! Our time and *God's* time
differs.

You are suffering because you fail to understand *God's* timing. When you don't understand *God's* timing everything you try to achieve is resulting into frustration and tears, due to the 'waiting period' for things to fall into place. Failure is a result of you doing something too early or too late, according to God's timing. You understand the economy, who to love, who to hate but you don't understand *God's* timing. You think *God's* time works similar to yours, which is why you move too fast in everything you do. Example: You proposed yesterday, after a week you already slept with that person, because in the heat of the moment, you thought it was the perfect time. Was it the right time for you, or was it *God's* time for you?

There are three things that make human beings lose focus of their God-given purpose. The first is lust, which in turn leads to death. *(James 1:15)*

The second one is the love of money. (*1 Timothy 6:10*) You stop doing *God's* work, because you are too busy making money. It is extremely dangerous to possess so much money; you don't know what to do with it, resulting in you starting to waste it. Money will end up being your boss. Instead of you being in control of your money; it will end up controlling you. It is at this point that alcohol, sex, cars, lavish clothing, start to become affordable to those who are being ruled by money.

It is also important to understand that lack of money could limit you to know *God* better; actually you can never progress to become the best in anything you do, when you need money to progress to the next level in your career. Money can help you to move forward in life, but even so, you must not allow it to rule your life.

Principles sustain everything in the world. You could achieve much in life, but without principles you are going to crumble down. It is extremely dangerous for you to be a Christian without principles. There exist principles that will teach and help you to become a good Christian leader. Principles exist to help you excel in every area of your life. There are also principles urging you to keep moving forward, even though you are faced with austere times. You desire to marry, run a business, prophesy, speak in tongues, but first you must master the Word of *God*, for that's wherein all principles are contained. You are now a Christian. How must you keep yourself? Principles only start working once you realise you are not poor but rich, not sick but healed, not last but first, when you become aware that you are a royal priesthood, a percular somebody, a chosen generation! (*1 Peter 2:9*)

Principles start working when you start questioning yourself: *"Am I in the right place? Am I doing the right thing? Is it the right time to do this?"* You should bear in mind that, a principle exists for winning, likewise for losing. The first principle you as a Christian should master is: Transformation. Yes, you are transformed, but are you able to maintain this change? From here on you need to become steadfast in your faith, no backsliding again. Do not cling onto your past. You will end up staying connected to it.

Practice integrity. Yes, you are a Christian, but can people trust you? Can you commit yourself to tithing, offerings, treating your body like a temple of the Holy Spirit? Do you possess that kind of integrity? Integrity helps you to practice self-control, and it helps you with your faith in *God*. It makes you respect *God* and the sphere of your contact (people you get in contact with daily), most importantly respect for yourself.

You need to grow, maturing from one level to another. When you grow in one level, you must show growth in every level. It may be in your business, marriage, job, ministry and family. The tendency is that most people don't grow. They still behave in the same way they did when they were still new converts. Growth is going to prevent you continuing with worldly things.

As a Child of *God,* you also need to gain clarity. Know what you are good at. Associate with greatness, with people who will challenge you, who will help you discover your gifts and talents. Clarity emphasises your true potential. You may be failing in life, because you have not yet discovered your potential. You must be prepared to work with God, to discover your potential. Allow Him to automatically unveil unto you, the way you are supposed to lead your life. Discovering your potential is actually discovering yourself. After you discovered who you are in Christ, follows resemblance.

Resemblance let people see *God* in your life. Allow your life to exhibit the love of *God.* Let people see the grace of *God*, His love in the way you lead your life. May they come and ask advice from you, because being a Christian means exhibiting the true character of *God*. You are unique and distinct; you are created to accomplish something that no one else can. You are responsible for stirring the gift of *God* that is inside you.

Most Christians are suffering from indecisiveness. Example: You are married to someone you don't love. It kills every vision or dream you have. Speak to your wife / husband, be honest. If she/ he wish to stay married, then you must both try your best to make it work, for *God* hates divorce. However, if your wife / husband wish to end the marriage, don't compromise, because there is someone out there whom you will love, and who will love you equally. Anything destructive needs to be removed from your life. Keep doing what *God* has called you to do. Every time you make a decision, do it publicly. Yet again you are busy doing things secretively. You are hiding something. You have a husband or wife, but you have a secret affair, you don't want people to know about.

Planning ahead makes everything go according to plan, therefore before you take action, make sure you plan first. Without planning you seldom succeed in anything you do. Planning ensures that success becomes part of your life. This only counts where it concerns *God's* plans, not your own mere plans.

Last but not least, you need diligence, for your destiny demands it. Obstacles may come against you, your vision, your purpose, but diligence will give you confidence and make you brave, to patiently persevere. When you understand *God's* principles, it becomes easier to understand His timing. You will never again pray for anything that is out of line with God's purpose for your life.

Your problem is that you have actually drawn a demarcation line in your life. You hold a stopwatch, when *God* doesn't bless you inside a certain time frame, you take a different route. You want *God's* timing to be your timing. This is why you fail dismally, for you always assume you are moving in *God's* timing, when you are not. People who wrote you off, don't possess power to write you back in, only *God's* timing will be decisive. Your 'now' and *God's* 'now' are totally different, likewise the physical 'now' and the spiritual 'now' aren't similar. People who are actually prophesying that you won't make it, or you will die, totally miss the point, only *God's* timing has the final say about your life.

The Bible teaches that *Hannah* prayed to *God* for a child, at that time *God* was looking for a prophet. *Hannah's* prayer was in line with *God's,* purpose, therefore *God* granted her the privilege to carry a prophet inside her womb. (*1 Samuel 1:10-20*) You have sinned and fallen short of *God's* glory, however *God* still protected you. You know why? He was protecting you because of the 'seed' He placed inside you. Understanding *God's* timing is vital for every Christian, as the answer in reaching your destiny, is hidden in *God's* timing. The Bible states: *'There is a time for everything under the sun.' (Ecclesiastes 3:1)* There is a time for every purpose in your life. You must know, *'many are the plans in a man's heart, but the purpose of God prevails. (Proverbs 19:21).*

Even in your own life everything must be done in its right season. You cannot plant a vineyard in the time when corn has to be planted. Your seeds will go to waste. That is why so many marriages, families and businesses break down. They were initiated during the wrong period of time. They were initiated with time that is measured by sight. The things of *God* do not work by sight, but by faith. You thought it was the right time for you to get married because you considered your age, and jumped to a conclusion before consulting *God.* You are now suffering the consequences of your hasty actions. You wish you could go back and undo it, but it's too late. Our time and *God's* time are two different things.

That is why, when there was a famine in the land of the Philistines, everyone was not thinking about planting, because the soil was dry, due to the fact that there was no rain. All the people thought it was time to eat that which they had, but *God* used *Isaac* in his time to do an extraordinary miracle. *God* commanded *Isaac* to plant, and everyone laughed at him, mocked him when he was acting upon what *God* commanded. Little did they know that *Isaac* was not acting on his own timing, for even unto him it was not the time to plant! Instead he was acting on *God's* timing, guess what? The Bible says that he reaped a hundred- fold, ain' that a supernatural miracle! (*Genesis 26:12 & 13)*

Our time has a demarcation line where it gets exhausted, and cannot perform more things for us. *God's* timing has no limitations, He is never too early neither too late, He is always right on time. As a Christian, pray that you don't do things because you feel like it, but because *God* commanded you. When you start understanding *God's* timing you won't be prone to fall into temptation easily. You will know when to speak and when to keep quiet. You will know when the right time arrives to get married, start a business, buy a house.

Everything about your life will have order. Time is the currency of life, be careful of time you waste now, for it is going to determine the outcome of your future. Time spent wisely shall guarantee you a bright and secure future. Be wise; understand *God's* timing. Prevent yourself from doing things in your own time!

CHAPTER 8

THE DEPOSIT INSIDE YOU

Guard the good deposit that was entrusted to you; guard it with the help of the Holy Spirit who lives in us. (*2 Timothy 1:4*) Everyone received a certain deposit that *God* entrusted them with. It is up to each individual to guard and stir that deposit, for the glory and purpose of *God.* You can never enjoy the things of *God* until you start to 'squeeze.' An orange can be so cunning and beautiful to the eye, but without squeezing it, one can never enjoy the sweetness. There is something that *God* deposited inside you, that's not about your face, hips, cleavage, chest or your 'six pack.' It's all about the inner you. Many people are good looking but act crazy. They speak as they please, date whomever they choose and above all; have limited riches to tangible things such as money and jewellery.

Don't you know that knowing *God* is richness? Before the foundation of the world, long before you were formed in your mother's womb, *God* already deposited something inside you.

You did so many wrong things: lied, stole, aborted, killed, fornicated; but *God* wants you to know that all those actions haven't disrupted what He placed inside you. You are failing to turn your problems into projects, because you are unaware of the potential inside you. It's not because you are smart, or intelligent, but it's because of what *God* deposited inside you. He chooses before we are born, what gifts and talents He wants to place inside each of us. What makes you unique, and the blueprint you are, is what *God* deposited inside of you. *God* is going to send a 'bee' into your life that is going to help you become fruitful. Whatever He deposited inside you can never function well, until someone enters your life, who will spur you into action. Afterwards the person will leave and move on, but not before he moved you, to start using the gifts and talents *God* placed inside you. Your blessings are not going to appear in millions, but in bits and pieces. One day you will possess much, and people will be surprised that you made it. The issue is that you despise the days of your humble beginnings. The Bibles says: *'Do not despise the days of humble beginnings.' (Zechariah 4:10)*

The worldly system limits the amount of money you withdraw from your bank account, likewise *God* is not pouring out all your blessings at once, for your 'heavenly account' will be left with an insufficient credit. Every time *God* calls you, He knows that He placed a deposit inside you. You have everything you need to fulfil your purpose, inside you. Where is *God* using you? Is it as a teacher, nurse, doctor or, mechanic? That is your training ground, for your duty lies within the Body of Christ.

'Then the Kingdom of heaven will be likened to ten virgins who took their lamps and went out to meet the bridegroom. Now five of them were wise and five of them were foolish. Those who were foolish took their lamps and took no oil with them. But the wise took oil in their vessels with their lamps. The bridegroom was delayed, they all slumbered and slept. And at midnight the cry was heard: Behold, the bridegroom is coming; go out to meet him! Then all those virgins arose and trimmed their lamps. And the foolish said to the wise, "Give us some of your oil, our lamps are going out' (Matthew 25:1-8)

The deposit *God* has placed inside you matures, just as money deposited into your bank account accumulates interest every day. Do not rush to use what *God* has given unto you, for you must first grow and mature in *God*. There are some things you must leave aside. The challenge is that you want to receive from *God*, but you don't want to let go. (*Luke 18:18-23*) When there is a deposit inside you, you will forfeit some of the things in your life. Your blessings are still fresh and untouched, whenever you want to withdraw, the first step is to forfeit the 'old' you.

Always remember, the depth of any foundation determines the height of the building. Do not attend church because you want prosperity, healing, marriage or employment, for to receive all the above you must first invest in God, by seeking His kingdom first, and then all the above will be added. (*Matthew 6:33*).

If you really need something from *God*, you must be prepared to sacrifice. What are you sacrificing to *God*, in order for you to start receiving from *God*? *Abraham* wasn't going to receive

God's promise, if he wasn't prepared to forfeit something that he held dear. *Abraham* was prepared to sacrifice his son *Isaac* to receive *God's* promise. (***Genesis 22:1-10***)

When *God* places a deposit inside you, it shows that He trusts you, for He knows your ability and potential! Why are you, a Christian, suffering? *God* wants you to start using the deposit inside you. Often people don't realise that there is a deposit inside them, that's why they are unable to resist the devil, until he flees. Your lack of knowledge concerning the Word of *God* makes it easier for the devil to kick you, left and right like a soccer ball. There is a deposit inside you, and *God* will show you everything in detail. Bear in mind that your deposit might never function fully around people who knows you well, therefore *God* may ask you to leave them behind, so that you could become fruitful elsewhere. There are some family members, and friends who do not show understanding regarding your deposit, therefore they don't support you. Your deposit can never function fully when you are still around them. Refer back to *Chapter 6*, where I wrote about leaving your comfort zone.

God saw that the deposit inside *Abraham* couldn't function while he was still amongst his people. He had to forfeit his family and country. (***Genesis 12:1***) Thus, your deposit can never function fully, unless tested in the things you love. You are a great person, but things are not happening for you, you haven't yet been stirred on the inside. If you truly believe that you have a deposit inside you, why is your life so unbearable, that it seems easier to give up, than to move on? You are longing for better education, a bigger house, new car, a husband or a wife. All the above is proof that there is a certain deposit inside you.

The *Lord* will mature your deposit, and tell the world about it, only after you start living according to His Word. *God* matures and prunes, cultivates and also waters. Whenever you deposit money into your bank account, you anticipate interest. The goodness of *God* is the deposit inside you, but alas you aren't living in His complete goodness, due to your ignorance and disobedience to *God's* Word. You can never turn your problems into projects when you lack knowledge about the deposit inside you. The gift inside you is going to open room for you, to stand before great men. **(*Proverbs 18:16*)**

Most people do not realise how powerful the pen could be. Write down every one of your visions, strategies and plans. Every time you wish to succeed, you must strategise and plan, for what you put on paper is what you are going to receive. Success doesn't come by luck, chance or miracle; it comes by faith and purpose. You are a spiritual 'machine' designed to see beyond where you are now, you can see your future. A vision is not a decision, it's a discovery. It possesses the knowledge of *God's* purpose and plan for your life. For a vision to be realised, you must pursue it, for it is your future and your success.

Do not rejoice in failure for you are giving the devil the upper hand, *God* created you to solve problems! Your vision is designed to fulfil someone else's purpose. You are a 'genius', you receive understanding from *God* who will renew your mind, to be fixed on those things *God* wants you to focus on. Do not live in a fantasy world, it's what you accomplish here on earth, that's going to support your judgement in heaven!

Vision makes a man great. Only those who risk going too far could possibly find out how far one could go! What costs you nothing, costs somebody else much, your ability decides your personal progress and productivity. Most people fail dismally because they don't plan. Planning creates order, order in turn, creates increase. You fail because you don't invest in *God;* therefore you are not a cheerful giver. It is more blessed to give than to receive. *God* created the poor, for you to help them rise. As a Child of *God* you may only have one talent, even so, you must strategise in different things. Beware being a jack of all trades and master of none! Many people with one talent cannot exploit, they already buried what *God* gave them. (*Matthew 25:18*)

Having a talent doesn't place you in charge. If you are in charge, then your talent in leadership opened a door for you, you were being faithful with your leadership skills. The deposit inside you will enable you to keep commitments. (*Daniel 1:3-16*) Often your deposit is not functioning well, because you fail to stay committed to *God.* Commitment is keeping your word and never wavering. When you stay committed to *God,* no matter how small or big, *God* honours it. He will make you to rise above everyone, not because you are smarter or more intelligent, more beautiful or handsomer but because you kept your word!

You are not advancing to a better and best way of living, because you committed adultery, steal, fornicate and lie, but mostly because you are not keeping your commitment to *God.* Understand that this works double-sided, you want things from *God,* and He wants you to be committed to Him. It's not about how much you pray, tithe, offer, speak in tongues, fast, but it's about the level of your commitment. The problem is; you don't do those things out of commitment, but out of obligation. Commitment doesn't need time for itself, it lasts a lifetime! It is a lifestyle. You are committed to your ministry, instead of being committed to *God*. Don't you realise that *God* honours pure commitment, but you are only committed to *God* when you need something from Him. After you received what you asked for, you become too busy to worship that same *God* who blessed you!

Pure and true commitment has no season, it is just simply commitment! Actually it is giving all of you without anticipating anything in return. You don't give it in order to buy something. It is done in public or private. It is vital to stay committed when no one sees your commitment. Unfortunately you only want to show commitment when everyone is watching you. Pure and true commitment brings results and favour from *God*. You would rather suffer than forfeit your commitment to *God;* you must stay committed even if it's not convenient.

The only reason *God* isn't enlarging your territory is because every time He does, you change your commitment to the blessings rather than Him, the Blesser. Yes, you are still in a predicament, but are you prepared to take a step forward, making up your mind to be, and stay committed to God only? You are good in making up your mind, but you act in a way totally different and contrary to your words. Pure commitment goes hand in hand with your actions. The best gospel is not the one you preach or read, it is the one you live! Start living for

God, then the deposit inside you, is going to create room for you to prosper and succeed amazingly!

CHAPTER 9

WHY, LORD?

"Why did I not die at birth? Why did I not perish when I came from the womb? Why did the knees receive me? Or why the breasts, that I should be nursed? For now I would be lying still and be quiet, I would have been asleep; then I would have been at rest with kings and counsellors of the earth, who built ruins for themselves. With princes who had gold, who filled their houses with silver. Or why was I not hidden in the ground like a stillborn child, like an infant who never saw the light of day?" (Job 3:11-16)

You don't choose where or how you fall. The road of life for so many Christians is so unbearable, that it seems easier for them to rather give up, than to move forward. It is during this time, when they are cast down, that they start to question many things: *"But, why Lord? Is it because there is no God? Is this the way it is going to end?" You get hurt by your family, in marriage, business, in your job and in health. Where do you go to seek help? Is your God with you at all times? When you fall down, when you rise again, when you are sick, when you get well, when you don't have money, when you have money, is God still with you?* You are failing to tap into the anointing of *God* because you are not on the same wavelength as Him .When the atmosphere changes, can you still go down on your knees and pray to *God? God's* wisdom is infinite; He is undoubtedly a wonderful Counsellor.

You are chosen by *God,* but whenever tribulations come your way, you forsake *God* and seek help from fetish priests or *inyangas.* Before you ask anything from *God,* why don't you first confess your sins and humble yourself before *Him?* When you are in trouble, which power do you enquire from? Before you do so, did you first check and cross-examined yourself? You pray, fast, offer, tithe and give generously; actually you do everything in your power, and *God's* power, but nothing changes in your life. The people who don't serve *God* have everything and all is going well for them, but what about you? Even a centurion, who knew nothing about *God,* didn't read the Bible neither attended church, found favour in the eyes of *Jesus Christ*; why? The centurion took a leap of faith, and that was why *Jesus* was prepared to listen when he spoke.

You attend church, read *God*'s Word daily, participate in all things that involve *God,* but when you speak to *God* it seems He hasn't got time to listen to you, why? After you have invested most of your time, surrendered everything to *God,* everything turns out like *God* has forsaken you. You question Him: *"But why?"* Know that every question has an answer. There is an answer to your every 'why? It might not come from a prophet, man, a relative, a policeman, but it may be lying right inside you. You ask yourself, why whenever you pray, you first have to suffer, before you receive an answer from *God? God* loves you even when you go through tough times. He allows suffering, pain, trouble and hardships because He knows how all these problems will end. *God* brought you to it; He will take you through it. Do you know why you pray and things don't happen? It's because you have never looked deeper to determine the root of your problem. Don't you know that there is an enemy that wants you to suffer, actually wants you to fall? He wants you to fail in life. Sometimes he may come as a friend. Even though you do well, the enemy can never say:*"well done."* An enemy purposefully delegates you wrong, he wants to frustrate and discredit you.

The devil will never succeed in testing *Jesus,* because *Jesus* used God's Word to defeat Satan. *(Matthew 4:1-11)* The devil wants to take away the things that bring joy unto you, but he makes a mistake by thinking that outward things bring joy into your life. The problem is that when the devil brings tricks to fight you, you also want to use tricks to fight back, instead of using the Word of *God,* for the Word is super-powerful. Stop doing things out of your intellectual knowledge, rather act by the *Spirit of God,* and the devil shall flee from you.

Overcoming the devil you must refuse any instruction from him, adhere to *God's* Word only. The devil tries to manipulate you, that your *God* given purpose may be forfeited. He wants you to think you are smarter and better than anyone. You waste time fighting ancestral spirits, witches, and wizards, instead of fighting with the devil himself, because he is the real problem causer, not sickness, poverty, pain, miscarriage, unemployment, inflation, recession or any other predicaments. You waste time worrying about useless things because you don't know where *God* wants to take you next!

As a Child of *God*, instead of asking *God*: *"Why?"* use your insight, have a vision that you run with. When I was a kid I used a 'vision book.' I would cut out luxurious pictures from magazines, things like cars, houses, clothes, and pasted them in that book, wherein I wrote the following statement: *One day I will own all these things.* Till today I don't own any, but I haven't stopped running with my vision. Do not worry how big it is; don't be scared up to the point you that compromise with the devil. The devil always wants to take you on top of a mountain; he makes climbing very easy, he just puts you into an elevator! However, *God* wants you to take it step by step, as long as you bypass certain stages, you will find yourself unable to endure.

The devil wants to give you something that's too big to fit into your pocket, to make you believe you own it. The reason why most Christians question *God* is due to the fact, that they are blinded to the things of *God.* They don't know what *God* has instore for their lives. Why is it you do everything according to the Word of *God,* but nothing takes place? Why is it that you tell lies when you mean to tell the truth? You mean to humble yourself but you swell with pride instead. You gather courage, only to tremble with fear, and you want by all means to live, but you find yourself among the 'dead.' Yes, water is for free, but when you are thirsty you buy yourself wine and vinegar to drink to quench your thirst but alas, the thirst isn't quenched. You walk in light but you are constantly surrounded by darkness.

All these things are happening in your life, and you are uncertain whether to continue worshipping *God* or not. Your life is moving towards a strange and unknown world, even in the midst of a crowd you feel lonely. You long to taste the result of prayer. You are desperately waiting for *God* to turn your life around. You wonder why He provides for the birds in the air, the fishes in the sea, however fails to provide for you? You observe the way they soar and squirm, but still *God* provides for them, you ask yourself: *"What does God value most, men or beast?"* You wonder why *God* isn't doing anything for you, even though He values you.

Everything about your life seems to be 'dead, your marriage, business, car, home, family, absolutely everything with and around you seems 'dead.' You show love towards people, but they don't love you in return, give but never receive anything back. You knock but not even a single door has ever opened for you, you sought but did not find. The most unfortunate part is that you ask but have never received. You start thinking that your life is useless, you have no reason for living. You wish that you could just disappear or become extinct, and then you won't have to face the challenges, staring you in the face right this moment. What you actually don't know, is that your enemy isn't wrong! He wants to make you suffer, steal from you, hurt and destroy you. He wants to beat you up and leave you for 'dead.' *(John 10:10)*

Your enemy has no techniques of his own. He copies from, or imitates other people, for he possesses no skills or creativity of his own. He runs after fame, but alas, he is not admired enough by the public. His life doesn't change, because he has no life of his own. The enemy knows your weaknesses; he is an enemy that keeps revisiting and accusing you. Sometimes you even wonder how the enemy can stand before the presence of *God*. Your lifestyle hands over the keys and authority to him. Understand that the devil is not wrong. His presence is causing you to keep running, because you want to avoid feeling more pain. If you were to go through life without any obstacles, it would cripple you. Troubles exist in order to keep and make you strong. Another question that arises is: *"How do I stop the pain?"*

Could the pain of losing your wealth, family, health, business, marriage, job, or whatever else you lost, go away? When you are in pain, no one advices you in what you should do. There is always a particular reaction to each kind of pain. Could the pain of losing what you treasure, stop? Why does pain emerge in the first place? No one orders pain, or goes out looking for it, but it comes your way unexpectedly. *God* allows pain to cross your path, for pain allows you to grow spiritually. Humble yourself before *God* when in pain, that His glory may be revealed through your pain. Pain is going to place you where *God* wants to use you. Pain and tribulation let the glory of *God* manifest. Pain doesn't go away because your friends support you or people sympathise with you. It stops when you remind yourself that *God* is in control.

Most Christians, when blessed tend to forget the Blesser. Be careful how you behave when *God* blesses you, don't wander far off, because pain will take you back to your former position. Why do you always turn towards *God* when you experience pain? Why don't you turn towards Him just because you love Him, and want to belong to Him? You need something from *God* however, have you ever promised Him anything? *God* doesn't want anything from you other than your heart, and you showing Him that you totally trust Him. Worship your way out of pain. Leave everything in *God's* hands. If you want to see *God* really provoked, worship Him with all your heart!

The principle to follow to get out of pain is much easier than you think. You need to put your heart into your effort. Every time you suffer pain, you get angry and look for the culprit who causes you pain, so you can avenge. When you are filled with revenge you start to hate even the people you aren't supposed to hate. Stop seeking revenge, crying, wandering around looking for witches and problem causers, because then you will fail to ever turn your problems into projects. Turn your face towards *God* and let Him take away the pain. Pain doesn't care if you are rich or poor, single or married, barren or fertile, educated or illiterate, you simply cannot close the door to pain, as it will cross your path no matter what.

For you to progress to another dimension, turn adversities into advantages, you need to pass through some pain. Yes, you are passing through pain –you have no money, you are barren and sick, but *God* wants you to be still and know that He is the *Lord.* Pain wants you to move and talk too much, you will start speaking negatively about yourself, and even worse, share your secrets with your enemy, but *God* wants you to be still. As long as you have the knowledge why you suffering pain, it is easy to be set free. Every time pain emerges, trouble arises, misery loves company! If you really want answers to your every 'why', you have to humble yourself before *God*. He shall lift you up in due time, thereafter your life will never be the same again!

It is important not to veer off God's track when passing through pain. This is where most of us lose it. When pain enters, you forfeit *God* and look for something that will ease your pain, but actually does not take it away. You become like the foolish wife of *Job,* who wanted her husband to curse *God* and die because of the pain he endured. *(Job 2:9)*

Fortunately *Job* was grounded in *God.* He understood that he couldn't worship and praise God only during good times, but also when things are bad. (*Job 2:7-10)* Through all his suffering *Job* never sinned; he remained faithful and steadfast before *God,* even while passing through pain. The main thing as a Christian is not passing through pain, but how you act when pain crosses your path. Do you curse and sin against *God?* Remain faithful and steadfast; *God* knows what He is doing. Continue praising and worshipping Him. He will not only ease your pain but, will completely remove it. Close your mouth and your heart. Don't inform everyone about your pain. Not everybody needs to know or hear about your pain, because there are some people who will use it against you.

It happened with *Jephthah* whose mother was a prostitute. (*Judges 11:1-3*) The community started using that knowledge against him. They labelled him with all sorts of evil names, even refused him to participate in anything concerning that particular community. It doesn't matter how, when, where and why you were born. Whether you like it or not, pain is going to be part of your life. Black or white, as long as you are worshipping the true living *God*, you will pass through some pain. You can never be a pure Christian without passing through some sort of pain. To become a pure Christian, you will be tested and approved. I know some of you know what I am talking about, for you have been tested financially, in marriage, physically, emotionally and also spiritually. To those of you still enjoying a 'test free' life, be warned, pain is on its way! In your marriage, business, family, job and body you are going to pass through pain until you are approved.

My beloved brethren in *Christ* bear this in mind: No pain, no gain! If our *Lord Jesus Christ* also passed through pain, who are we to be exempted from pain? I plead with you neither to lose hope, nor to surrender in times of pain, for there is always hope in our *Lord Jesus Christ*.

'Weeping may endure for a night, but joy comes in the morning' (*Psalm 30:5*)

CHAPTER 10

WHAT IS PRAYER?

"If my people, who are called by My name, will humble themselves and pray and seek My face and turn from their wicked ways, then I will hear from heaven and will forgive their sin and will heal their land" (2 Chronicles 7:14)

What you say with your mouth must come from your heart, likewise what you do. Don't say something with your mouth that doesn't tally with your actions. Being double minded is the opposite of holiness. What you do and say means a lot to *God.* What is prayer? Prayer is speaking the mind and purpose of *God.*

Sometimes Christians' commitment to *God* could be measured by a ruler. They worship *God* whenever they feel like doing so. Prayer is a principle that governs the Children of *God.* In every culture or religion, prayer is accepted as a greeting. People pray in many ways, but don't always understand it. You pray, but stay confused for your prayers have never been answered. Many people pray without believing, without faith, and then ask themselves: *"Does prayer really work? Does prayer make any difference? Does prayer get listened to by someone?"* After asking all these questions, they still kneel down and pray once more.

Why is prayer necessary? Why pray to *God* in the Name of *Jesus*? *Jesus* is the doorway to reach *God;* you cannot be in right standing with God, if you don't go through *Jesus Christ*. It's not through ancestral spirits like *Buddha, Shembe, Mohammed, Baal,* or *Mary,* but in Jesus Name. *Jesus* is like the blood flowing in our bodies. Why is prayer not answered according to your specifics? Most people think it's because they are sinners, or this and the other, but it's not about all of that. Sometimes you pray for money but *God* doesn't give you money, instead He answers in another way, not according to your specifics. Prayer is being eloquent, for it's not only *God* who will be listening, even the devil will be paying attention. It is speaking, what is in the spiritual realm to be manifested into the physical. It is an acceleration of *God* granting you your needs, because He knows what you need, even before you ask.

When do you stop praying? Who are the people who qualify to pray? Prayer is to understand God's mind and purpose, believing *God's* Word without a sign of doubt. The reason why your prayer life is not affective could be that you are praying out of line with God's purpose. When you start understanding *God's* mind, you will start receiving answered prayers daily. Prayer is a result of *God's* established authoritave structure between heaven and earth. Prayer affirms and confirms *God's* faithfulness. Prayer is simply respecting *God's* authority. Prayer is when man allows *God,* to let heaven come and intervene on earth. If you want *God* to do something for you, you must initiate the first step.

Prayer is a rightful tender and when you start understanding it, you will suffer less and experience less sorrow. Prayer is not an option, but a necessity. Once you begin praying, you will possess power and authority over everything. A necessity is something you cannot live without, just like prayer. As a Child of *God* you cannot function at *God's* junction, if you don't pray or understand how prayer works. In prayer it's all about position and relationship. Example: Without heaven earth can never be complete, likewise without earth, heaven cannot be complete. Prayer can do everything and anything. Some people don't know what to pray for, or when to stop praying. For your prayers to be affective, you must first understand why *God* created you the way you are, then you will have insight in what to pray for. You receive unanswered or 'wrong' answers on your prayers, because you lack knowledge in why *God* created you. When you pray don't stop praying, whether you received an answer or not, continue praying, also remember thanking *God* for answered prayers.

Many Christians end up questioning *God's* character, and start rebelling, as a result of unanswered prayers. The bigger question is: *"What do we lose by not praying?"* Misunderstanding how prayer works results into very pessimistic prayer results. You don't grow as a Christian, and you are often easily defeated. The worst part is that you don't qualify to be an heir of the Kingdom of Heaven, as you don't have any relationship with *God.* You lose direction, for prayer is never begging *God,* but rather being one in mind, soul and body with *God, then* your prayers will touch and move *God.*

When you don't understand *God,* it shows that you are not in an intimate relationship with Him. *God* wants you to know Him, when you do, you will realise that your pain and suffering doesn't make Him happy. Prayer without anticipating results could be misunderstood and lead to unanswered prayer. You are unable to turn your problems into projects, because you misunderstand how prayer works. Prayer must consist out of the truth and the biblical principles found in God's Word.

True prayer builds intimacy with *God*; it brings honour to His nature and character. Always act smart and be pure, because cleanliness is next to Godliness. Your prayers stay unanswered, because your lifestyle doesn't resemble *God. This* could be one of the main reasons when you call on *God,* He doesn't grace you with His presence. When you pray, pray and continue to pray, for you exhibit the true character of *God* which causes others to respect His integrity. Prayer enables you to believe in *God* and his Word and affirms His purpose and will. Prayer should be answered, or else *God* would not have taught us how to pray, or urged us to always pray for everything in every situation.

Your approach to *God* must be seasoned.

You must pray to gain understanding in the deeper and hidden things about your life, family, job, business, home and marriage. You pray to *God* because you are redeemed. *Jesus Christ* is our model, for He is what we are supposed to be. *God* gave us free-will starting from the beginning of everything. You can never enter into the presence of *God* if you are still controlled by free-will. For you cannot choose *God*, but *God* chose you and called you out of darkness, for in Him there is no darkness at all. There is only holiness that is prescribed to be the 'passport' to enter into the presence of *God*. Whenever you pray it is your spiritual position that matters to *God*. As Children of *God*; without understanding prayer, it is impossible, to function at *God's* junction. Prayer is a daily meal that you mustn't skip. Prayer may seem, and sometimes is calm and silent, but it's a very effective weapon for anyone who wants to walk on forbidden waters!

CHAPTER 11

WALKING ON
FORBIDDEN WATERS!

During the fourth watch of the night Jesus went out to them, walking on the sea. And when the disciples saw Him walking on the sea, they were troubled, saying," It's a ghost!"And they cried out in fear. But immediately Jesus spoke to them, saying "Be of good cheer! It is I; do not be afraid." And Peter answered Him and said "Lord, if it is You command me to come to You on the water." So He said "Come." And when Peter had come down out of the boat, he walked on the water and came towards Jesus." (Matthew 14:25-29)

As a Child of *God* you were born with something unique, a gift from *God*. What is this gift you were born with? Your gift is going to create room for you, and lead you to the doorway of success and overflowing blessings. (*Proverbs 18:16*)

The gift doesn't belong to you but to *God*, don't brag about it. (*2 Corinthians 4:7*) The gift inside us has been placed there, for us to display and exhibit *Christ* with our lifestyle. Why then are most Christians not able to turn their problems into projects? It is because you are not bold enough to walk on forbidden waters. What is inside you that will reveal *God's* glory in your life? Don't expect the gift to make everything going smooth, for as long as you will be in this world, trouble is going to cross your path, but the question is how are you going to 'trouble' those troubles? Most Christians suffer because they give up easily when things are tough. Are you unaware that it is just a set-up strategy to make you stronger and teach you endurance? The gift of *God* inside you will start to grow and mature in the things of *God.* What would you be holding when *Jesus Christ* returns? You cannot use the gift of *God* for yourself only, you are king over your gift, but you can never last on the throne if you misuse it. When you don't work with or stir the gift of *God* inside you, you can never walk on forbidden waters, thus your problems can never be transformed into projects. *'Guard the good deposit that was entrusted to you-guard it with the help of the Holy Spirit who lives in us.' (2 Timothy 1:14)*

What did *God* place inside you? Have you made any profit out of it? Your gifting is your assignment even so, it doesn't belong to you. You are extremely necessary, you may not know it, might not look like it, but you are the solution and answer to your problems. Your assignment is not hard, for you are not alone, *God* is with you.

There are things that you inherited from your family lineage, due to your blood connection. In your family there is a distinctive pattern, which your great grandparents, parents and other relatives failed to break. Your lineage is identified by prostitution, stealing, fornication, drug abuse, barrenness, unemployment and poverty. For you to be able to walk on forbidden waters, you firstly need to identify and recognise your bondage. You are being haunted by foundational curses. Every wrong thing that is presently identifying your life, you saw it happening to your parents. You saw your mother fornicating, your father being a criminal, your sister aborting and not getting married, your mother consulting witch doctors, you brother dropping out of college. You saw it then, now it's repeating in your life. You are not suffering because of sin. It's not that you don't pray or fast, you are suffering due to foundational curses. How strong is the foundation of your money, job, family, business, marriage and education? Foundational curses are responsible for causing confusion in your marriage, business, job, family and other areas of your life. When you find yourself in a pit, you don't need sympathy. You don't need someone who comes with logistics, who will ask you how you fell in the first place. You don't need self-pitying, charismatic or 'holy' people, neither those speaking about hope, you need actual help. Someone who will pull you out and up, but help will never come your way, unless you shout or scream. *'But when he saw the wind was boisterous, he was afraid; and beginning to sink, he cried out, saying:"Lord, save me!"' (Matthew 14:30)*

Being called a Christian won't make the devil run away from you. You will never be able to convert your problems into projects unless you start walking on forbidden waters. Yes, your father died without owning a house, car or company, but as a Child of *God*, someone who is extraordinary, you must try convincing yourself that you will get married, have children, drive your own car, own a house and run your own businesses. Yes, in your family no one ever achieved this, but you are different, for you are chosen by *God*. *(1 Peter 2:9)*

The world is filled with modern technology, internet dating, mxit, and twitter, Facebook, Whatsapp and Google. People meet on dating sites, and fall in love before they even meet in person. Tell yourself that you will make it come rain or shine, '*if* **God is for you, who can be against you?' (Romans 8:31)** There are three things you are supposed to do, before you maybe could manage to turn your problems into projects; thus before you would be able to walk on forbidden waters.

The first one is: Listening to, and obeying the command of *God*. *Peter* only got out of the boat after being given the authority to do so, by *Jesus Christ*. (**Matthew 14:29**) You are suffering either because of your ignorance, or either because you acted too fast before hearing *God's* command. When you act out of *God's* command, it becomes extremely easy to function at *God's* junction. Whenever you take action without hearing from *God* first, you're destroying your blessings. It is very important to listen, obey and follow *God's* command.

The second thing is: As a Child of *God* you should always be prepared to take risks in life. Regardless the prevailing situations around you, are you bold enough to turn to the *Lord?* Can you take a leap of faith when you are faced with 'dead' situations? The woman at Zaraphath took a bold risk. She faced severe famine when she was approached by the prophet *Elijah,* who asked her to prepare the last meal for him, and only afterwards could she think about herself and her child. Amazingly she did as the prophet of *God* commanded her, and miraculously she never ran out of food, why? She was prepared to risk her and her child's lives, to save the prophet's life.

1 Kings 17:13-16- Elijah said to her: "Don't be afraid. Go home and do as you have said. But first make a small cake of bread for me, from what you have, and bring it to me, and then make something for yourself and your son. For this is what the Lord God of Israel says: 'The jar of flour will not be used up, and the jug of oil will not run dry, until the day the Lord gives rain on the land.'" She went away and did as Elijah had told her. So there was food every day for Elijah, and for the woman and her family. For the jar of flour was not used up, and the jug of oil did not run dry, in keeping with the Word of the Lord, spoken by Elijah.

What about the four lepers who risked entering the enemy's camp, looking for food? *2 Kings 7:3& 4-Now there were four men with leprosy, at the entrance of the city gate. They said to each other: "Why stay here until we die? If we say,' we'll go into the city-the famine is there, and we will die. And if we stay here, we will die. So let's go over to the camp of the Arameans, and surrender. If they spare us, we live; if they kill us, then we die.'"* Wasn't that boldness and greater faith in action? At some point in your life you have to reach a point, whereby you become as radical as you can possibly be.

You keep on telling yourself that whether you live or die it doesn't matter, what matters are that you want to go to the *Lord*. When I look at *Peter*, I see a man who was bold enough to take a risk, regardless the situation inside the boat, or outside on the sea. Yes, inside the boat it was no longer safe, but it was much safer compared to the roaring waves in the open sea, the cracking of thunder and lightning bolts, as the storm worsened. I think the other disciples tried to hold him back, they could have said: *"Are you out of you mind? Do you really believe that this ghost is Jesus? What if it's a scam or set-up of the devil? Rather stay in the boat; do you think it's possible to walk on water? Peter you are a fisherman, possibly acquainted with the up-thrust laws of motion in physics? Why do you have a death wish?"*

During your life people might ask you the same questions. *"How are you planning to succeed, when your whole family lineage thus far failed?"* Tell those people boldly, that you don't know yet, but what you do know, is that you are following the Lord's command. Like *Peter,* you must climb out of your boat; your problems, predicaments and troubles, and take a step towards *God,* regardless the anticipated consequences.

The third one is: Commitment. You need to commit yourself to the fullest, if you serious about turning your problems into projects. *Peter* started off smoothly, but when he was only a hand reach away from *Jesus*, he started sinking. Understand, the storm was not a challenge whilst *Peter* stayed focused on *Jesus*. It became a problem as soon as he shifted his focus away from *Jesus,* unto the huge waves. This is the problem most Christians are faced with, when they only one step away from receiving their miracle, they shift their focus away from *God*. *(Matthew 14:30)*

You must remain committed to *God* no matter the odds, for commitment should not be measured by visible things. Commitment is simply commitment. Don't sink because austere situations are crippling you; rather sink because you remained committed to *God*. Your faith must stay unwavering. *God* is where He has always been. You are the problem; you are the one who veers off God's track, thinking *God* left you. *God* stays in one place, but due to lack of commitment and consistency, you lose focus of *God* ending up not knowing where He is.

Walking on forbidden waters needs people who are grounded in God's Word. Everyone wants to repeat what others once did, however when you want to turn your problems into projects, you must be willing to start doing things never done before. Stop being a photocopy of someone else. Begin to be the master copy of yourself, a great original. Every time you venture into business, it is similar to someone else's. Truth is: The fact that Mr X is making it in a particular field does not automatically mean you will be successful in that particular field. You will find Mr X making profit and you running a loss, you know why? Mr X is doing what he loves, but you are copying him.

When all the Israelites were busy praying to *God* to give them victory against their enemies, a man who was prepared to walk on forbidden waters prayed for something new and different. *Joshua* prayed for the sun to stand still, and it did for almost the whole day. The Bible is clear; for it records that there was no day like that before or after. It only happened with *Joshua,* and only on that particular day. (*Joshua 10:13-14*) People walking on forbidden waters are those harbouring a different Spirit. When everyone is seeing a problem, they see a project in the making. It is well documented in the lineage of your family that not even a single person, believes in *God.* Sadly you are afraid of being different therefore you also follow in their footsteps, even though deep in your heart you believe in *God.*

Nowadays there are parents whose children don't attend school, just because they themselves never attended school. This wasn't due to a lack of money, but education was taboo to them, because they believed school would be disrespecting their ancestors. Some men run polygamous families, because they believe in the lie that a real man is depicted by the number of women he marries. You are aware of this lie, yet you continue, only because all the men in your family have more than one wife, and you are not prepared, or you are too afraid to be different. In simple words: you are not prepared to walk on forbidden waters.

Walking on forbidden waters demands you to be a prayerful person. How can we be sure *God* hears us when we pray? *"Then you will call upon Me and come and pray to Me, I will listen." (Jeremiah 29:12*) In the worldly system there exist rules, regulations and rights. In prayer we don't have rights, rather an obligation to pray for one another. We all have to obey rules and regulations, for rules maintain order. Prayer works differently, for the rules in prayer are not rules like the laws of a country, but guidelines in how to pray. *God* grants us as His children spiritual authority, in which we must grow as Christians, to reach spiritual maturity. We don't have rights, or receive rights from God, but we do receive spiritual authority when we become *God's* Children. Anyone may pray, for *God* listens to the prayer of a righteous man, who prays with a sincere heart.

Here follow some examples: The Lord's Prayer is a good example of how we must pray **(Matthew 5:5-14).** Remember also people like: *Abraham, Isaac, Jacob, Hagar, Daniel, Hannah, Esther, Samuel, David, Hiskia, Elijah, Elisha, Jesus* and so many others. They all prayed with sincerity, it resulted in God hearing, listening to and answering their prayers.

Rights grant certain people privileges that others don't have. Example: Citizens of a country have rights immigrants don't have. Prayer is therefore not a Christian's right, but as Children of *God,* we are obligated to pray about everything, and to continue praying and not grow tired. As Children of God we have spiritual authority in Christ, that same authority, we have to put into practice when we pray, then our prayers will bring forth change, it will move *God's* hand into action, and we will receive answers to our prayers – not always the answer we anticipated! *(Philippians 4:6, Colossians 4:2, 1 Thessalonians 5:17 & 18 & Isaiah 38:1-8).*

You will find yourself unable to walk on forbidden waters if your life is not governed by prayer. Yes, you pray, however you don't understand your spiritual authority, and as a result lack knowledge in how to put it into practice, therefore your prayers stay unanswered. When *God* placed *Adam* and *Eve* in the Garden of Eden, He gave them spiritual authority to subdue and dominate over all creation. **(Genesis 1:28)** Unfortunately the devil came and robbed them of that authority, even though they gained knowledge to distinguish between good and evil. *Adam* and *Eve* did not know that *God* created them to be like Him, they did not need to eat forbidden fruit to become like *God,* for *God* created *Adam* and *Eve* to His Likeness. He created man to have relationship with Him. We, as people are related to *God,* because we are created in His Likeness. *Eve* believed a lie. She believed *Satan* when he convinced her to eat of the fruit, for the fruit will make them be like *God,* but unbeknown to them, they were already like *God,* being created in His Image. *(Genesis 1:27 & Genesis 3:4-6)*

In the Garden of Eden, they were given the privilege of enjoying abundant life. *Adam* did not have to work in order to survive; *God* created everything *Adam* would need to live in abundance, before creating him. It is after he lost his spiritual authority, that we read he will have to till the ground in order to survive. *(Genesis 3:19)* That same spiritual authority is going to make you walk on forbidden waters.

To walk on forbidden waters is to break your mould and stand out from the crowd, only if you are in right standing with *God,* then He will use you to accomplish great exploits. We all have a certain power within us wherein we tend to doubt. You have been wonderfully and fearfully made. *(Psalm 139:14)*

May this book help you think about what's happening in your life. Take a moment to do serious introspection, determining where you find yourself, and where you strive to be. As you walk on forbidden waters do not be distracted by the things surrounding you, as it may lead to your drowning.

My beloved brethren, I thank you that we could read this book together. I hope it blessed you the way it blessed me. My prayer is that when you are down, and your soul is weary, the good *Lord* may raise you up to walk on forbidden waters!!

www.ingramcontent.com/pod-product-compliance
Lightning Source LLC
Chambersburg PA
CBHW052125090426
42741CB00009B/1960